Brigitte Reck

Between Democracy and Technocracy

The Role of Expertise for the European Parliament

Brigitte Reck

BETWEEN DEMOCRACY AND TECHNOCRACY

The Role of Expertise for the European Parliament

ibidem-Verlag
Stuttgart

Bibliografische Information Der Deutschen Bibliothek

Die Deutsche Bibliothek verzeichnet diese Publikation in der Deutschen Nationalbibliografie; detaillierte bibliografische Daten sind im Internet über <http://dnb.ddb.de> abrufbar.

∞

Gedruckt auf alterungsbeständigem, säurefreien Papier
Printed on acid-free paper

ISBN: 3-89821-236-X

© *ibidem*-Verlag
Stuttgart 2003
Alle Rechte vorbehalten

Printed in Germany

To Wolfgang

Acknowledgements

This analysis on the role of expertise for the European Parliament has been developped as a master thesis at the College of Europe in Bruges in the academic year 2001/2002. For this publication the content and composition of the study remained the same. In some points however small corrections and changes have been made, concerning mainly the updating of information.

First of all, I would like to thank the "EUROPÄISCHE BEWEGUNG DEUTSCHLAND" and the ADOLF WÜRTH GMBH & CO for providing me with the scolarship which made it possible for me to study at the College of Europe. My acknowledgements go then to Prof. Dr. Rudolf HRBEK for his academic framing and supervision of the analysis within his reseach seminar. I would also like to express my sincere gratitude to Prof. Dr. NEUNREITHER for his kind support in conceptionalising the academic questions and his helpful suggestions and comments on the subject.

And last, but not least, I dedicate my deepest thanks to all my interview partners in Brussels, MEPs and officials, who allowed me to get an interesting and enriching inside view of the European Parliament on my research questions. It should however be noted, that due to time constraints no complete representative survey on the issue could be made.

Table of Content:

4 The European Parliament's resources in terms of expertise and legislative assistance

ABSTRACT

The starting point of this analysis is the perception that the European Union is increasingly facing a dilemma between democracy and technocracy or, in the words of Robert Dahl: between "system effectiveness and citizen participation" (DAHL 1994). On the one hand, the EU is today accused for lacking sufficient democratic legitimacy, and on the other, it is true that public policy-making is getting more and more complex and technical, and that politicians are for that reason to a high degree reliant on the technical knowledge of specialised experts. The main argument of this study is that the European Parliament, being the only directly legitimated body within the institutional set-up of the EU and thus the symbol of democracy, plays a key role in bridging this gap.

The main focus of this book is thus the role of expertise for the European Parliament. It is assumed that, in order to fulfil its new challenges posed by its enhanced role in EU decision-making, the European Parliament depends to a high degree on internal and external help in form of expert knowledge, policy advice and parliamentary assistance. The centre of attention is thus dedicated to the question on which internal and external sources of expertise the European Parliament can rely on and to what extent the Parliament has adapted its internal capacities to the new challenges.

It discovers, mainly on the basis of interviews with politicians and officials in Brussels, that the European Parliament, although being aware of the adaptation pressure arising mainly from co-decision but also from enhanced complexity, has not reformed its internal structures to the new situation. It is argued that the European Parliament's internal capacities of expertise and support are still organised along the needs of the pre-Maastricht era and are thus not well equipped to meet the new challenge. In contrast, lobby groups were increasing their efforts to influence the European Parliament the introduction of the co-decision procedure by offering MEPs their technical expert knowledge. They have in such way filled a vacuum, which evolved with the non-adaptation of the European Parliament's internal structures to the new requirements in terms of expertise. In other words: the insufficient "independent" in-house capacities, made the Members of Parliament more dependent on expertise gathered form outside and thus also to a certain extent more captive for private interests.

In this dependency on external information and knowledge, which is always to a certain extent biased, lies a serious danger for European democracy. Being aware of the fact that independent resources of information and expert knowledge have become in today's complex society a key instrument for political institutions to influence policy, this study suggests that the European Parliament needs to be well equipped with these fundamental resources, in order to be capable not only to fulfil its new legislative tasks, but also to control politically the European Commission, which is rather known for its technocratic policy-making. It could, in such way play a key role in bridging the gap between democratic control and good quality outcomes.

1 INTRODUCTION

The difficult ratification process of the Maastricht Treaty has revealed that the state of democracy in the European Union is in crisis and has been at the origin of an immense literature on the so-called "democratic deficit". Theoretical analysts have not only criticised the technocratic forms of policy-making in the European Union, but also drawn attention to a constant decline of parliamentary democracy. Public policy-making in the European Union is, however, getting more and more complex and technical, and politicians are therefore to a high degree reliant on the technical knowledge of specialised experts. An apparent dilemma is arising between technocracy and democracy, or, in the words of Robert Dahl: between system effectiveness and citizen participation (DAHL 1994). The European Parliament, being the only directly legitimated body within the institutional set-up of the European Union and thus a symbol of democracy, plays a key role in this respect. It seems thus interesting to analyse the role that expertise plays for the European Parliament.

The evolution of the European Parliament has been marked by a continual increase in its powers. Starting out as a purely consultative body composed of representatives delegated from the national parliaments, over the decades the European Parliament saw its powers extended with each major Treaty reform. In the aftermath of its first direct election in 1979, the European Parliament itself pushed successfully for an upgrading of its role, drawing advantage from its new democratic legitimacy. In this way, it has enhanced its position vis-à-vis the other two principal political institutions of the European Union: the European Commission and the Council of

Ministers. Milestones on the way to its new position were the Single European Act, the Treaty of Maastricht and the Treaty of Amsterdam.

With the introduction of co-decision, the European Parliament has become an important player in the Union's decision-making process. This gain in political power constitutes for the European Parliament a major challenge, in regard to its parallel increase in responsibility for the legislation adopted or rejected and the workload to manage. As a result of the "spill-over effect"[1], the European Parliament, additionally to the challenge of its enhanced political weight, also has to deal with completely new and complex policy issues. Through this two-folded increase in power and in competencies, the European Parliament is also confronted with an inexorable increase in workload and responsibility. Furthermore, the issues at stake have become more and more technical and complex.

This paper is based on the assumption that it is becoming more and more difficult for Members of the European Parliament to understand and deal with these increasingly complex and sometimes highly technical matters. It is assumed that, in order to fulfil the new challenges posed by its enhanced role and increased complexity in the decision-making process, the European Parliament depends to a high degree on internal and external help in the form of expert knowledge, policy advice and parliamentary assistance. This leads us to the question of whether the European Parliament has the necessary resources and support for tackling these new challenges. This

---

[1] "Spill-over" refers to the way in which the integration in one economic sector creates pressures for further integration in related sectors and policy areas. The concept of "spill-over" and "functional pressure" is part of the neo-functionalist theory with its main proponent Ernst B. HAAS.

study will examine which internal and external sources of expertise the European Parliament can rely on and to what extent the Parliament has adapted its internal capacities of expertise and assistance to tackle the new challenges of increased responsibility, workload and time-pressure.

Before coming to answer these leading questions, a first chapter will include theoretical considerations on the relationship between technocracy and democracy with particular regard to the European Union. This will provide a theoretical basis for the discussion on the role of expertise for the European Union with a special focus on the European Parliament, which plays a key role in this respect.

Chapter two will then analyse the role of the European Parliament within the institutional set-up of the European Union and especially its recent developments. It will mainly focus on the new challenges the European Parliament faces today.

Finally, the third chapter will investigate, on which internal and external resources in form of expertise, policy advice and parliamentary assistance the European Parliament can rely in order to confront its new challenges. This major chapter will be divided in two parts. The first will deal with the parliamentary in-house capacities, while the second will reflect on which external resources of expertise the European Parliament can access.

The first part will thus explore, whether the European Parliament has sufficient in-house resources in terms of expertise necessary to respond to its enhanced role and how far it has adapted its internal structures and its in-house resources to the new situation. This study is based on the premise that, if the European Parliament has an eventual structural weakness in this respect, this may make the Parliament especially dependent on external information and expert knowledge and perhaps also more subject to capture by the influence of lobbying groups. It is also presumed that such a structural weakness as the insufficient "independent" in-house expertise will prevent the European Parliament from making full use of its powers.

The second part of this third chapter will analyse which possibilities of access to external expert knowledge the European Parliament has. There is a general assumption that Parliaments are in general at a disadvantage in this respect towards the executive organs and that this is especially true of the European Parliament in relation to the Commission. Does the European Parliament have a structural weakness in terms of access to expert knowledge? The aim of this section will be to test whether this is really the case.

2 THEORETICAL CONSIDERATIONS

2.1 Technocracy in the European Union

The political system of the European Union is often accused of being ruled
by technocrats and experts who ignore the basic thrust of democracy. Already the early stage of European integration was marked by a technocratic
approach, the key idea of the Monnet plan for the ECSC being the pivotal
role given to experts in the making of supranational public policy: the High
Authority should be composed of selected experts. Monnet prefigured a
system of "*engrenage*" whereby networks of interest groups, organised la-
bour and firms affected by European policy would be gradually involved in
the public policy making (RADAELLI 1999: 30). Still the today's European
Commission being responsible to initiate policy proposals is particularly
open to external expert advice. It not only attracts but also organises a
dense network of consultation. In order not to become too dependent on
expert knowledge provided by the member states it includes all kinds of
private interests in the process of policy formulation. The specialised individual Directorates General of the Commission have over time established
close links to relevant interest groups and created issue-specific networks
that possess the characteristics of "epistemic communities" (HAAS, P.
1992).

Before going into further discussion on why the EU policy-making process
might have a tendency to be rather technocratic, it seems worthwhile to explain briefly the basic concept and the fundamental characteristics of technocracy. Technocracy can be described as a "system of governance in
which technically trained experts rule by virtue of their specialised knowl-

edge and position in dominate political and economic institutions" (FISCHER 1990: 17). Although there are numerous different theories on technocracy, some basic elements are generally seen as fundamental to the concept, mainly the use of "technical expertise". Technocracy refers to the adaptation of expertise to the tasks of governance and to governmental decision-making that is designed to promote *technical* solutions to *political* problems, whereby technical knowledge serves as the base of power. The technocrat believes that rational analysis and scientific examination of facts will bring about unanimous consensus on policy solutions. By contrast, he feels uneasy under conditions of political conflict and ideological debates (RADAELLI 1999: 37). Politics on the other hand has to do with values and believes, and no algorithm will ever provide an answer to the confronting values and ideologies. Technocracy is thus to a certain degree equivalent to de-politicisation and stands in a certain conflict to democracy.

How can it be explained that the EU policy process is rather technocratic and based on efficiency? This feature can be perceived as a consequence of the specialisation of the European Union as a political system in producing regulatory policy. While nation-states developed and consolidated around distributive and redistribute policies, basically welfare and taxation, the European Union has mainly specialised in technical policies, especially in regulation, whereas distributive policies have been less important than the regulatory dimension (MAJONE 1996). The European Union has as political system a comparative advantage in the production of regulation, as the resource of regulatory policy-making is based on knowledge rather than on budget. Regulatory policy, aiming at efficiency, is more suitable for discussion and for negotiation in expert circles, whereas redistribution kindles the passions of politicians, political parties and the mass opinion. Regulation is the type of policy that suits better the expertise, the tendency towards technical negotiation and the general avoidance of open political debate.

2.2 Expertise and Politics

The relationship between science and policy has been described as "an unhappy marriage" (COLLINGRIDGE/ REEVE 1986, pp. 1–6). Indeed, knowledge and power are deeply intertwined in European public policy. Although technocracy is not the best characterisation of the European Union, knowledge plays a crucial role in public policy-making of the European Union. Political scientists have detected a dramatic increase in the political power of expertise, and this is especially the case for EU politics. The real challenge for the European Union is thus how to combine an increased politicisation with the need for more expertise. Politics and knowledge, which are normally seen as polar opposites, are indeed needed at the same time for developing public policy in the European Union.

The European Parliament plays a key role in tackling this challenge of bridging the gap between expertise and politics, as it is the *political* institution, whose duty it is to politicise the legislative proposals elaborated by the Commissions technocratic expert circles. While the Commission as the executive body has a well-defined policy, which is to a high degree driven by expertise and scientific advice, and holds communities of experts and *"copinage technocratique"* between Commission's officials and experts (RADAELLI 1999: 7), the European Parliament is rather marked by plurality and differing interests. It should thus add a political and democratic element to the technocratic way of policy-making of the European Commission. Its role is hence to politicise the issues at stake and to take political decisions between policy options with pros and cons.

However, as the European Union lacks the necessary political infrastructure between the elected and the electors as well as a European-wide public demos and opinion, the European Parliament, in order to gain precedence over competing positions, will not launch a political debate trying to persuade a broad public. It will rather be based of expert knowledge (KOHLER-KOCH 1997: 3). Those who command superior information on what is considered to be appropriate and efficient in common problem solving have persuasive power. As a matter of fact, the European Parliament needs to equip itself with more expertise, in order to do informed choices and be influential in the decision-making process.

2.3 Technocracy and Democracy: a European dilemma?

The idea of policy analysis and technocratic decision-making has been criticised for undermining democratic society. Experts have increasingly - so it has been argued - come to form a powerful elite within government and society, so much so that the influence of analysts poses more of a threat to democratic decision-making than a means of improving it. Giovanni Sartori has put forward that given the complexity of issues confronting policy-makers, the expert's opinion must acquire much greater weight than his vote as an elector (SARTORI 1962). It is today true that information and advice of technical experts has become a key resource in the governance of modern society, and that politicians who are in most cases not specialised experts themselves, are highly reliant on expertise. It is the access to this technical knowledge and skills that sustains the power of the technocratic elite. And, conversely, it is the lack of access to such knowledge that hinders the possibility of an active and meaningful involvement in the political decision processes for a large majority of the public. In this sense, one is right to argue that knowledge is power (HAAS, E. 1990).

It should however be noted that technical experts are not in direct political control and that this lack of democratic control constitutes a real threat for democracy. This is why European policy-making is very vulnerable to criticism focusing on what is called "the democratic deficit". The question to pose is thus what are democracy's chances in the face of this technocratic threat and can democracy work in a complex and highly differentiated society? This study is based on the believe that the European Parliament, being the only democratic accountable institution in the institutional framework of the European Union, should play a major role in controlling politically the technocratic policy-making circles in the European Union, mainly through its function to scrutinise the European Commissions legislative proposals. However, in order to be capable to do so, it requires having independent resources of expert knowledge and strong internal structures of policy advice and parliamentary assistance.

In the democratic theory, a basic difference is made between *input-* and *output*-based democratic legitimacy. Whereas technocratic policy-making, which is based on knowledge, scientific expertise and efficiency, relies thus on *output*-legitimacy, representative and parliamentary democracy is based on *input*-legitimacy. Robert Dahl identified a democratic dilemma between system effectiveness and citizen participation (DAHL 1994). Although there is indeed a certain tension between democracy and expertise, they should nevertheless not be seen as a choice of "either/ or". While the European Union is very strong concerning its output legitimacy, there is still much to improve on the input legitimacy. Whereas the twenty Commissioners are nominated by their governments, and the members of the Council, though chosen by the democratic procedures in force in their own countries, do not have a direct electoral mandate for their European role (HOLDSWORTH 2000: 202), the European Parliament is the only directly legitimated body of the European Union. The Parliament fulfils, within the institutional set-up, the task of scrutinising the proposals and actions from the Commission. It has thus a key role to play in the regain of the democratic legitimacy of the European Union, adding an element of political control and scrutiny to the technocratic policy-making style of the Commission.

The European Union has been described as the prototype of "post-parliamentary governance" where experts, large organisations and sectoral networks with the involvement of public and private actors represent the essence of modern governance (RADAELLI 1999: 3). Indeed, European governance is based on direct participation of affected interests in policy networks. Hence, in this view, expert sovereignty tends to prevail over popular or parliamentary sovereignty. Andersen and Burns have pointed out that the European Union is based on three mechanisms of representation: *expert* representation, representation of *interest groups* and diffuse interests in policy networks, and *national* representation through the presence of member states in the EU policy process, whereas *parliamentary-territorial* representation, on the other hand, is less developed (ANDERSEN/ BURNS 1996: 230). One of the main reasons for the marginal role parliamentary democracy is that societies have become highly differentiated and far too complex for a parliament to monitor, acquire sufficient knowledge and competence, and to deliberate. Moreover, politicians lack, in general, the legal, technical and specialised knowledge and skills essential to the tasks at hand. Andersen and Burns have thus argued that the high level of expertise necessary to participate in European public policy does not make the system amenable to traditional parliamentary oversight (ANDERSEN/ BURNS 1996: 229).

This argument is based on the assumption that parliaments are weak in dealing with highly technical matters and that they do not have enough (access to) expert knowledge in order to be influential in European policy-making. This consideration could, however, also be seen through different lenses. If we agree, on the one hand, with the assumption that EU policy-making is, as a result of its regulatory nature, highly dependent on expert knowledge and if we share, on the other hand, the value of parliamentary democracy, we should see the need for the European Parliament to equip itself with the means to influence public policy, which lays in the capacity of independent expertise. This study is based on the assumption that the European Parliament plays a fundamental role not only for the democratic legitimacy of the European Union, but also as an instance for bridging the gap between democracy and technocracy. The next chapter will therefore analyse the state of the European Parliament, its changed role within the institutional set-up of the European Union and the challenges it faces today.

3 THE EUROPEAN PARLIAMENT: AN INCREASINGLY IMPORTANT PLAYER IN EU DECISION-MAKING

3.1 From consultation to co-decision

The evolution of the European Parliament was part of the overall process of European integration as it developed in the 1980s and 1990s. Milestones in the integration process as well as in the development of the European Parliament's powers were the Single European Act, the Maastricht and the Amsterdam Treaty. As the integration process has proceeded, the European Parliament has acquired new powers, which enhanced its position vis-à-vis the other two principal political institutions of the European Union: the European Commission and the Council.

At its origins the European Parliament was composed of delegations from national parliaments and had merely consultative functions on a small range of legislative proposals. These powers were considered as too limited, especially from those who estimated that the European Communities suffered a "democratic deficit". The European Parliament did fight, since its creation, for more participatory rights in EU decision-making, and it did so with a degree of success. Over four decades, the European Parliament has moved from being a purely consultative assembly to being a genuine co-legislator in a European Union that has itself evolved considerably both in scope and in powers. In 1979, European Parliament was for the first time directly elected by universal suffrage. This event has been crucial for its further evolution and role within the institutional triangle. Not only did it provide Parliament with full-time members, but it did also provide for greater democratic legitimacy. Henceforth, it could take advantage of its direct legitimacy to ask for more legislative participation.

The Single European Act introduced two new legislative procedures, which enhanced Parliaments powers. The so-called *"co-operation procedure"* added a second reading to the traditional consultation procedure and gave the European Parliament a suspensive veto right. This means that Parliament can in second reading reject the Councils common position, which then fails unless the latter overrules Parliament by unanimity within three months. Parliament had now also the possibility to press for amendments, which, if supported by the Commission, can only be rejected unanimously in the Council of Ministers (CORBETT et al 2000: 4). The Single European Act also enhanced Parliament's rights in requiring Parliament's *assent* for the ratification of accession treaties and association agreements.

A further major step in the European Parliaments pace of constant increase in legislative powers has been the Treaty of Maastricht, which introduced the so-called *"co-decision procedure"*. This new procedure was based on the co-operation procedure, but with two important additional innovations, which constitute a qualitative difference to pure consultation and co-operation: first, the inclusion of a formal conciliation committee with the task of negotiating a compromise between Parliament and Council, and second, the option for the Parliament to definitely reject the decision of the Council, thus causing the legislation to fall. If, after two readings each, Council and Parliament have not agreed the same text, the matter is referred to a conciliation committee composed of equal numbers of each side. This Committee has the job of negotiating a compromise text to be submitted for final approval to the European Parliament and the Council. The main innovation of the co-decision procedure is the European Parliament's power to reject definitely a common position by the majority of its composing members. In this event the Council can't impose upon the European Parliament and the proposed act is deemed not being adopted.

For the first time, the European Parliament is acting jointly and on an equal basis with the Council, mainly in Community activities related with the establishment and functioning of the EC internal market. The Council can't impose itself on the European Parliament anymore, as the agreement of both institutions is necessary for the adoption of a legislative act. This marks an important change for the inter-institutional relationship between the two legislative bodies, as the Council can't neglect Parliaments opinion anymore.

As a result of these innovations, there has been an increase of informal inter-institutional linkages, especially between the Council and the Parliament. In order to anticipate the opinion of Parliament in its common position, the Council is now interested to contact the European Parliament very early in the legislative process. Thus, there has been a considerable expansion of informal inter-institutional dialogue between the Council and the European Parliament.

However, the co-decision procedure, in its initial form after its introduction by the Treaty of Maastricht, has been criticised for mainly three deficits: first of all, for its limitation in scope. After Maastricht co-decision applied to 15 areas of Community action, amounting to about one quarter of legislative texts only. Furthermore, the co-decision procedure has been described as "lengthy and cumbersome" and "opaquely complex" (WESTLAKE 1994: 144). Comprising two readings by the European Parliament with the possibility of a third reading, the co-decision procedure was estimated being too time-consuming: the time span for the second and third readings takes a minimum of fifteen months. The procedure has also been criticised, especially by the European Parliament itself, as still "unfairly balanced" in favour of the Council (WESTLAKE 1994: 144).

3.2 The "new" co-decision procedure under the Treaty of Amsterdam

One of the major achievements of the Amsterdam IGC 1996 has definitely been the reform of the co-decision procedure. The Treaty of Amsterdam did respond directly to the aforementioned criticisms and deficits of the co-decision procedure in its initial form. It brought important innovations to co-decision basically through an extension of its scope of application as well as through the simplification of the procedure, so that the European Parliament is today a genuine co-legislator on equal footing with the Council in a large number of areas.

3.2.1 Extension of its scope of application

The Treaty of Amsterdam has essentially widened the field of application of the co-decision procedure. When first introduced by the Maastricht Treaty, co-decision applied to 15 areas of Community activity, amounting to about one quarter of the legislative texts that pass through Parliament (CORBETT/ JACOBS/ SHACKLETON 2000: 191). The Amsterdam Treaty has extended this list by 8 new and to 15[2] old Treaty provisions. The European

---

[2] Including the new provision on the free movement of persons (Art. 67 par. 3 of the new title IV EC), which will apply after five years.

Parliament is thus after the coming into force of the Amsterdam Treaty co-legislator under 38 areas altogether, including some central legislative powers of the European Union, such as most common market-related provisions (the "four freedoms"), and at least some types of decision in most other policy areas such as transport, the fight against fraud, development co-operation, environment, etc.

The Amsterdam Treaty has replaced the co-operation procedure by co-decision in nearly all cases, except the Economic and Monetary Union (EMU). As a result, co-decision can now be perceived as the normal legislative procedure, covering more than half of Community legislation. The extension of its scope of application in Amsterdam has been impressive and did finally put the European Parliament on equal footing with the Council in a large number of areas. This led many observers to the conclusion that the European Parliament can be called the big winner of the IGC 1996/ 97. Parliament is now adopting EU legislation jointly with the Council, having equal rights and obligations.

Giving an overall assessment of the extension of European Parliament competencies under the Treaty of Amsterdam, it can be argued that a crucial psychological step has been made: it is thus likely that co-decision will henceforth be perceived as the future standard procedure, with consultation and co-operation soon being considered as the exception to the rule. This might in future, make it easier to switch to co-decision as the single legislative procedure at a later IGC (FALKNER/ NENTWICH 2000: 30).

It should however be noted that through this enhancement of its role, the European Parliament gained also more responsibility for the legislation adopted and had to tackle an important increase in workload. The extension of co-decision to other important policy areas lead to a huge increase in the total number of dossiers dealt with under co-decision procedure, which increased by a factor of 2,5 in a full year. In the year following entry into force of the Amsterdam Treaty, 65 cases of co-decision were concluded (BARÓN CRESPO 2000: 1). As much as these figures demonstrate the increased influence of Parliament, this means also increased workload for the European Parliament, and especially for the respective Committees and rapporteurs concerned.

3.2.2 Simplification of the procedure

Apart from extending the scope of co-decision to other fields of application, the Treaty of Amsterdam also simplified the procedure itself considerably, making it more efficient and less time-consuming. Basically it omitted the third Council reading and introduced the possibility of bringing co-decision dossiers to a conclusion at the end of the first or at second reading (COUNCIL 1999: 1).

This latter innovation, opened up by Art. 251 TEC, has been a major element of reform. It formally provided for a closure of the procedure already at first reading, if Parliament and Council find an agreement. If Parliament for example does not amend the Commission's proposal or if the Council accepts all European Parliament amendments, it may adopt the act at this very early stage without having to adopt a common position. This innovation has considerably altered relations between the institutions, especially those of the European Parliament and the Council (COUNCIL 2000: 7). This new provision for the swift adoption of co-decision acts has made it necessary for new informal contacts and negotiations between the two co-legislators.

34

Similarly, if the European Parliament approves the Council's common position during its second reading, it can vote the text into law without need to refer it back to the Council. Furthermore, if, in its second reading, the European Parliament does not take a position within three months, the act is also deemed being adopted in the version of the Council's common position.

Also the third reading has been changes in such a way that the Council may no longer seek to impose its original common position after a failure of the conciliation committee, unless the European Parliament overruled it by an absolute majority of its members. Under Amsterdam, both institutions share responsibility for the adoption as well as for the failure of a proposed legislative act, putting the European Parliament on equal footing with the Council also in this stage of the procedure.

The reform of the co-decision procedure with regard to efficiency also provided for stricter time limits to assure that the period between the second reading and the outcome of the whole procedure does not take longer than nine and a half months.

The Amsterdam Treaty with its innovations for the legislative procedures can thus be interpreted as in line with the previous IGC's, each of which brought the EU decision-making structure closer to a federal state model with a parliamentary and a state chamber, however, a unique type of federal decision-making. Given that the Amsterdam Treaty extends the application of the co-decision procedure to many new areas, the Intergovernmental Conference 1996/97 may be interpreted as a major step toward a bicameral legislative authority in the European Union where Parliament and Council jointly adopt legislation, the approval of both being necessary

(CORBETT/ JACOBS/ SHACKLETON 2000: 188). "Classical two-chamber legislature: in which the Council represents the states and the European Parliament represents the citizens" (HIX 1999)

The European Parliament gained more political weight throughout its history, being more and more involved in the decision-making process of the European Union. This enhancement in legislative influence and political power, increased also its responsibility and workload.

3.2.3 Informal "Trialogues"

As a result of co-decision a new legislative culture has gradually evolved between the two co-legislators, a culture of inter-institutional co-operation, negotiation and compromise, with the support of the Commission in its role as mediator. Parliament and Council recognised that they need to work in close co-operation and that they cannot afford to stay isolated, one from the other, as in the co-decision procedure no act can be adopted without the agreement of both institutions. As both institutions have an important interest in reaching an agreement at an early stage in order to avoid the time-consuming conciliation procedure, they are inclined to have a much more intense inter-institutional contact early in the procedure.

Council and Parliament now, in partnership with the Commission, take their respective positions and constraints into account in the course of their work. The Council, being aware that under co-decision it can't impose its decisions on Parliament anymore, tries to take Parliaments position as much as possible into account, while drafting the common position. Having experienced lengthy and difficult conciliation negotiations, the Council is no more willing to try to come to a deal before the common position and sometimes even before first reading (BARÓN CRESPO 2000: 2). Similarly, Members of European Parliament might be inclined to anticipate the Council's views on the issue while drafting their amendments in order to get the approval of the governments already at first reading

The increase of its formal powers strengthened the European Parliament's position in contacts and discussions with the other institutions, which became more and more important with the extension of the European Parliament's legislative powers. With the entry into force of the Amsterdam Treaty and the increased importance of co-decision Parliament is exploring reinforced forms of dialogue with the Council. It changed its rules of procedure to allow the Council to come before its committees in person and comment on draft amendments, to present its common position to the committee responsible and to enter into dialogue with the committee chair or rapporteur to look for possible compromise amendments at second reading (CORBETT/ JACOBS/ SHACKLETON 2000: 203).

Once the main lines of the positions have been established, informal tripartite meetings, attended by the Council, European Parliament and Commission, are organised to clarify positions, identify areas of difference an discuss compromises. These so-called *"trialogues"* are essential to an exchange and better understanding of the respective positions, to the airing of difficulties and to the identification of areas of disagreement, as well for the purposes of negotiation. The original aim of "informal trialogues" was at the time of Maastricht co-decision procedure to prepare for Conciliation Committee meetings. The institutions agreed, yet, that in view with the aim of quickest possible closure of the procedure, tripartite meetings between the Council, European Parliament and Commission are needed throughout the procedure. Thus, this innovation has been extended under the "new" co-decision procedure of the Amsterdam Treaty to include other - earlier - co-decision stages, as it is expressed in the Joint declaration of 4th May 1999.

3.2.4 The Inter-Institutional Agreement of May 1999

When the Amsterdam Treaty came into force, Council, Commission and the European Parliament signed the Joint declaration on practical arrangements for the co-decision procedure of 4th May 1999. This inter-institutional agreement is an important statement of the three institutions, which paces the way for the fastest possible conclusion of the legislative procedure. It calls for the adoption of a co-decision acts at the earliest possible opportunity and encourages inter-institutional contacts necessary for completion of legislation as quickly as possible:

> "Appropriate contacts may be established with a view to achieving a better understanding of the respective positions and thus to bringing the legislative procedure to a conclusion as quickly as possible";
> "The institutions shall co-operate in good faith with a view to reconciling their positions as far as possible so that wherever possible acts can be adopted at fist reading." (JOINT DECLARATION 1999)

The aim behind the intention to shorten the procedure is to make co-decision more effective in view with the extension of its scope of application. In view of trying to find an agreement already after first or second reading, the Joint Declaration stresses the need to extend the informal inter-institutional contacts, known as "trialogues" or "tripartite negotiations" to earlier stages of the co-decision procedure:

> "The European Parliament, the Council and the Commission, […], note that the present practice of contacts between the Council Presi-

dency, the Commission and the chairmen of the relevant committees and/or the rapporteurs of Parliament and between co-chairmen of the Conciliation committee has proven its worth. The institutions confirm that this practice should be extended to cover all stages of the co-decision procedure." (JOINT DECLARATION 1999)

The Treaty of Amsterdam and the Joint Declaration of 4th May 1999 mark, as we have seen, a decisive trend towards adoption of co-decision dossiers as quickly as possible. This trend can already today be perceived in empirical data. Since the coming into force of the Amsterdam Treaty first and second-reading agreements have become frequent. They occur with about 75% of all co-decision dossiers. Nearly 25% of dossiers were concluded at first reading. A little over 50% were concluded at second reading following Parliament approval of the Council's common position or after Council approval of the EP's amendments to the common position. Finally, 25% were concluded during conciliation (COUNCIL 2000: 8). These figures were quite different before the Amsterdam Treaty innovations, since under the Maastricht co-decision procedure nearly half of all dossiers ended up at the conciliation stage (COUNCIL 2000: 9).

This development towards the earliest possible closure of the co-decision procedure is a decisive one. On the one hand, this new approach has made it easier to deal with the extension of the scope of co-decision at least in terms of time-management. It has enabled the institutions to cope with the increase in the total number of co-decision dossiers (COUNCIL 2000: 8).

Yet on the other hand, this trend towards earliest possible adoption of co-decision dossiers resulted in a sizeable new workload and a greater time-pressure for the European Parliament. Mainly since the coming into force of the Amsterdam Treaty and as a result of the aforementioned Joint Declaration of 1999, Parliament had much less time to deal with a co-decision dossiers, to scrutinise the Commission proposal, consult expertise, form an opinion on the subject, dialogue with the Council and make amendments. That means that Members of Parliament, and especially the rapporteurs, had not only more workload through the increased number of co-decision acts, but they also had to work much quicker than before, what means once again increased workload. Parliament has today in a large number of policy areas only some months time to work on highly complex subjects and to recruit expertise on the subject (Interview MERSCH 2002).

This new tendency, initiated by the Amsterdam Treaty and the Joint Declaration, towards speedier adoption of co-decision acts has resulted in a considerable increase not only in workload but also in time-pressure on the European Parliament, and particularly on the respective Committees, where the most important part of the legislative work is done. There is now less time for the rapporteur to write a report. Furthermore, not only has the number of legislative proposals to be dealt with every year more than doubled, but as a matter of fact the number of meetings and contacts at every level, which are essential to the follow-up and success of the procedure, has also risen sharply. The Council, being aware of the possible consequences, states that the quality of the legislative drafting must not suffer from these developments:

„The pursuit of first- and second-reading agreements on a large number of dossiers involves difficulties, for which solutions must be found" (COUNCIL 2000: 3). "Faster adoption of co-decision acts may not be at the expense of the quality of the procedure or of that of the legislation" (COUNCIL 2000 11).

The very tight deadlines should not have the result that the drafting of legislation is of a lower quality. In order to ensure sound drafting quality, this tendency to ever-swifter adoption of co-decision acts should be equilibrated by an increase in personal resources (A grades).

3.3 Developments in European Integration

At the same time, as the European Parliament gained political weight, other new policy sectors have come to a greater or lesser extent within the scope of the European Union's competencies. The economic project of the completion of the internal market entailed functional pressure to integrate other internal market-related, sectoral policy fields. This "spill-over effect" to new and complex policy fields had the effect that the European Union, and also the European Parliament, as it gained in political power, got involved in more and more policy fields, which are often very complex and highly technical areas. Examples being environmental policy, consumer protection, public health, Trans-European infrastructure networks, Research and Development (R&D), culture and vocational training. Each specific policy area requires specialised technical and often scientific expertise and engage multiple interests and groups with special concern or interest in the particular, specialised policy matter.

Environmental policy is a good example for such a complex policy area, where Parliament gained more and more influence. Treaty changes after the mid-1980s increased the European Parliaments role in environmental policy making. The Single European Act has formally introduced environmental policy at EU level in 1987, whereas Parliament participated through co-operation. With the Treaty of Maastricht, Parliament gained co-decision

41

rights in environmental policy, consumer protection and public health. The Treaty of Amsterdam, by extending co-decision to virtually all non-fiscal environmental measures, further enhanced the Parliaments bargaining position in environmental policy making (PETERSON/ BOMBERG 1999: 188). Decision-making on environmental policy issues is, by its very nature, highly technical and driven by scientific expertise. There is thus an increased need for expert knowledge in order to be capable to deal with these highly technical issues. As a matter of fact, Members of Parliament, who have in most cases no specific expert knowledge on the highly technical and sometimes even scientific questions, are to a certain degree dependent on outside expert knowledge.

Over the last decades, Parliament has not only gained more political influence and thus responsibility, but it has also gained more competencies in a large number of new policy areas. As a result, Members of Parliament have to deal nowadays with much more complex and technical policy areas. This new challenge leads, once again, to increased workload, as well as to dependency on expert knowledge and policy advice.

3.4 The new challenges of the European Parliament

As demonstrated above, the role of the European Parliament within the institutional set-up of the European Union has undergone considerable changes. Parliament not only gained considerably in political weight and influence on the decision-making process of the European Union throughout the last decades. Yet, as much it gained in decision-making powers, it also carries more responsibility for the legislation adopted or for the failure of a legislative act. As a result of these recent developments, the European

Parliament faces today as a "triple challenge" of increased complexity, workload and time pressure:

First of all, Parliament has to deal with an increased number of subjects, since new policy fields have been transferred in EU competencies, especially since the coming into force of the Single European Act in 1987. As these new policy areas are in most cases highly technical, Parliament challenges increased *complexity pressure*.

Second, Parliament gained in political weight and legislative participation, especially through the introduction of the co-decision procedure in Maastricht and the extension of its scope with the Treaty of Amsterdam. The huge increase in co-decision dossiers dealt with each year entail for the European Parliament and especially for the respective Committees and rapporteurs, an important increase in *workload pressure*.

Third, since the Inter-Institutional Agreement of 4th May 1999, which called for the earliest possible adoption of co-decision acts, Parliament is confronted with stricter time limits. It has today even less time to deal with a co-decision dossier. As a result, in addition to the increased workload, Parliament also has to work even quicker. Thus, the third challenge Parliament faces as a result of the recent developments is *time pressure*.

The effect of these trends has been to increase and often to alter the work of the committees of the European Parliament (HOLDSWORTH 2000: 204). Their work has steadily gained in salience. The introduction of co-decision enhanced the importance of the European Parliament's sectoral committees, in which most of its work has always been done. This increased workload has been detected by MEPs especially since Maastricht with the introduction of co-decision. As Parliament has now more responsibility on the legislation adopted, it also needs to work more cautiously. The augmented workflow, combined with an increase in complexity of some decision-making procedures, has certainly not increased the time available to committees and their members for the scrutiny of the dossiers (HOLDSWORTH 2000: 204).

Additionally, through its gain in salience, committees are more and more under external pressure, as lobbyists have intensified their efforts to influence Parliament. As a matter of fact, the committees work in an environment that is characterised by heavy pressure from outside: political and economic pressure, workload pressure and simple pressure of time. The environment, in which the committees are working explain the reasons for the need of qualified assistance and policy advice, as the quality of the legislation does depend on the expert knowledge and assistance the Members enjoy.

4 THE EUROPEAN PARLIAMENT'S RESOURCES IN TERMS OF EXPERTISE AND LEGISLATIVE ASSISTANCE

Due to its enhanced role and impact in European decision-making and its responsibility for the legislation adopted, the European Parliament has to tackle not only increased complexity but also an important workload and time pressure. If the Parliament is capable to manage these new challenges and to maintain, or even to increase its impact on the content of legislation, depends to a high degree on its resources in terms of technical expertise, policy advice and parliamentary assistance. This chapter will therefore analyse as well the internal structures and resources of the European Parliament as also the external resources of information and expert knowledge. The leading questions will be if the European Parliament reached to adapt its internal structures to its new situation and if it has the right resource allocation, in view of the increased power and workload?

This analysis will make a distinction between in-house and external resources of information and expert knowledge, following the theoretical public policy approach of David W. PARSONS (1996). Decision-making involves in this view four categories of sources, distinguishing internal and external and formal and informal resources. The use of formal and informal *internal* sources includes all kinds of knowledge generated within the institution. This may be the outcome of departmental research or inquiry, or through the use of special research or policy units, or formal internal reports generated by in-house experts or advisers. In several countries there are for example 'cabinets' of advisers, composed by a mixture of civil servants, academics, party activists, business people and industrials, which support individual ministers with policy advice of a formal and informal kind (PARSONS 1996: 386).

On the other hand, there is the knowledge that is generated wholly or in part *outside* the respective institution. This may be in the form of reports, or research and evidence form commissions or committees of inquiry, panels of experts, or other consultation. External policy advice may also be generated through informal discussion and conversation, rumour, intuition, gossip and so on. (PARSONS 1996: 386).

4.1 In-house capacities of the European Parliament

This chapter will analyse in which way the different parliamentary services can support the legislative work of the Members of Parliament, how well they are equipped to fulfil their respective role and if they have been adapted to the new challenges evolving from Parliaments increased role and salience in EU decision-making, which are basically its increased workload, time pressure and complexity. Finally, some recommendations are made, how these services might be revised, in order to be better adapted to the direct needs of the members of Parliament.

4.1.1 Parliamentary Assistance of the Civil Service

4.1.1.1   DG II for Parliamentary Committees and Delegations

There are mainly three parliamentary services that could provide for direct legislative assistance for the Members of Parliament: DG II for the Committees and Delegations, DG VI for Research and Documentation, and the newly established Legal Service of the Parliament. The Directorate-General for Parliamentary Committees and Delegations (DG II) organises the work of the 17 standing parliamentary committees, the 14 joint parliamentary committees and 20 inter-parliamentary delegations.

Since most of the DG II officials are directly attached to and work directly in the secretariat of a committee, this Service has become, since its very beginnings, the pivotal element in providing direct legislative assistance within the European Parliament (NEUNREITHER 2002: 8). The Secretariats of European Parliament committees normally have between two and seven administrators under a head of division, most of them being working now in Brussels. It is here, where the real parliamentary assistance takes place. The Committee staff have an important role in briefing members of the past activities and positions adopted within the Committee, help in background research for rapporteurs, give them advice and assist them in contacts with the Commission. When a rapporteur is nominated he or she can freely choose which assistance he or she would like to have. It happens quite frequently that officials from the Committee secretariat are drafting reports for the rapporteurs (Interview SCHMID 2002).

The full-time staff of the Parliament's committees is very small compared to the US Congress, but not to the national parliaments of the Member States (CORBETT et al 2000: 111). Although the overall size of this service amounts to only 10% of the whole staff, you find there the highest concentration of A grade officials, about 150, amounting to 40% of this category (NEUNREITHER 2002: 7). Officials of the committees' secretaries are coming from different scientific fields, yet they frequently tend to be generalists rather than specialists, largely because they are so few in number that they have to cover a wide range of policy areas.

As DG II is the service that is most directly involved in the legislative work of the Members of Parliament in the committees, they are the ones, who are facing most directly - together with the private staff of the MEPs - the increased legislative workload since Maastricht and Amsterdam. That is the reason why the European Parliament should have increased the workforce of this directly involved service in order to guarantee good quality legislation. However, if you analyse the development of the European Parliaments civil service staff policy in the early years of European integration and what direction it took recently, it does not at all make sense with view to the increased role and workload Parliament faces today.

Since the Assembly's beginning in 1952, there has been an enormous rise in the number of Parliament's staff. The figure did rise from 37 posts in 1952-1953, to 1995 by 1979, 2966 by 1984 and is now by over 4000 (CORBETT et al 2000: 171). This considerable increase in personal resulted from the increase in number of MEP's from 78 to over 600, the increase in working languages from four to eleven, the rise in the number of working languages from four to eleven, the rise in the number of nationalities from six to 15, and finally: the increased range of Parliament's responsibilities. Paradoxically, over the last 15 years, there has been a determined attempt to keep the overall numbers of permanent staff in check. Already in June 1983 Parliament voted for a freeze on the size of its establishment plan over the following four years. Yet as in the mid-80s Spain and Portugal had joined the Community, this was not possible, but the rate of increase in the number of Parliament staff did slow down (CORBETT et al 2000: 171).

The Committee on Budgets, in particular, has been consistently reluctant to provide the appropriations necessary to finance extra posts. It insisted in 1993 and 1994 to establish priorities and even to identify areas where there could be staff cutbacks (CORBETT et al 2000: 171). Despite the inevitable demands posed by enlargement in 1995 and the increased workload of the European Parliament since the introduction of the co-decision procedure, Parliament decided not to increase the number of permanent civil servants. Instead of new recruitment, Parliament sets on redeployment of existing staff, to meet new tasks.

4.1.1.2   DG IV for Research and Documentation

The Parliament's Directorate-General for Research (DG IV) consists of two Directorates: A: the Research Services, including the STOA unit[3] and B: the Parliamentary Documentation Centre, including analysis and docu-mentary research, archives, and information services. The Research Serv-ices are designed to support the European Parliament and its various bodies - the Presidency and the Bureau; committees and delegations; political groups; individual members and its staff etc. - with more detailed research on relevant policy issues.

The parliamentary research service provides mainly two different types of specialist briefing. In a first place, it does "long-term research" that provide for in-depth studies of about 50–60 pages in length. These are either carried out "in-house" - that is by the staff of the Directorate itself - or by external academic and research bodies. Additionally, "short-term briefings" of around 20 pages, which are usually prepared within the Directorate, are made available. These take a variety of forms and range from published

---

[3] As the STOA unit plays an important role in the assistance of the Parliaments legisla-tive work, this study will address it in a separated chapter.

papers for general distribution, to documentation and notes prepared on direct request of individual Members of Parliament, committees etc.

On request, the research services compile, in conjunction with the "documentalists" of the Parliamentary Documentation Centre, *dossiers* on particular subjects: for example on new proposals for EU legislation. These "info-packs" bring together, for example, brief outlines of the issues that are prepared by the research services themselves; or official documents from the Commission, Parliament or the Council; articles in the press; references to academic studies; and so on. These dossiers are, however, for only limited distribution, notably to chairmen and rapporteurs. But they can be made available for wider distribution, e.g. within the committees.

DG IV includes 30 researchers who produce background studies, briefings and notes in response to requests notably from the President, the committees and the delegations (CORBETT et al 2000: 170). Research service staff, as they are specialists in their field, is also available for advisory and other work. In particular, they co-operate with the secretariats of parliamentary committees to provide background briefing for rapporteurs and notes on a broad range of issues, gathering information from a network of researchers in parliaments in Europe, known as the European Centre for Parliamentary Research and Documentation. Since 1990, a programme of studies requested by the committee chairmen is agreed annually including items to be sub-contracted to external organisations such as universities, research institutes etc. (CORBETT et al 2000: 170). Under pressure of MEPs the Library facilities in Brussels have been developed substantially in recent years with a large selection of journals, books and newspapers as well as a growing number of staff able to respond to requests for information (CORBETT et al 2000: 170).

This sounds quite impressing. However, while comparing these theoretically described functions with reality, the picture looks a bit different. Indeed, the Research Service does actually not respond to the new challenges of the European Parliament, evolving since the mid-eighties. It is today still organised along the necessities of the time before Maastricht (Interview SCHMID 2002). There is a need to adapt the Research Service to the new requirements of the Parliament. Some deputies and committee presidents are recently pushing for more short time briefings are provided. What a Member of Parliament can get today is, on the one hand, quick information form the internet, and on the other hand, long term studies produced by DG IV or STOA, which are important as a background for understanding the issues at stake.

The deficiencies lay rather in a lack of mid-term studies. The European Parliament does not have an advice structure, which would make allowance for the MEPs real needs, which are to get technical and scientific advice within two weeks. It should therefore create an external advice structure, consisting of university and research institutes, a circle of policy advisers as contractors, which would provide Members of Parliament for quick responses in a short time period of 14 days (Interview SCHMID 2002). Especially the so-called "long-term studies" produced by DG IV staff in Luxembourg have too long time periods, especially in the technical area. Maybe in short future some changes will take place, as the DG IV is at the moment being evaluated by a consulting firm. The final report is going to be published in July.

Another deficiency of the DG VI is the separation of the "documentalists" which are located in Brussels and the "researchers" working in Luxembourg. This division does not make any sense in the eyes of the Vice-

President of the European Parliament, and should therefore be removed. What is instead needed, is a team of experts for each specific policy area consisting of documentalists and researchers together, as for example an "environment-team", consisting of researchers *and* documentalists, which are both specialised in environmental issues (Interview SCHMID 2002).

The European Parliament also needs more scientific staff in DG IV, which understands the technical language of the research studies that are coming in from external contractors and which is able to transfer it in a language that is understandable for non-scientists like the majority of the Members of Parliament. These problems have been identified so far, as the Vice-President of the European Parliament stated (Interview SCHMID 2002). The European Parliament has recognised the pressure to equip itself with the means to work seriously. However no concrete action has yet been undertaken in this direction (Interview SCHMID 2002).

4.1.1.3   The Legal Service

A further service of the European Parliament, which is growing in importance, is the Legal Service that has been created in 1985. The legal service staff is often consulted for its view by the committees, especially in disputes over the legal base of Community legislation (CORBETT et al 2000: 171). The most significant developments in its work result from the co-decision procedure. Under this procedure the European Parliament is, jointly with the Council, responsible for adopting, signing and publishing the final text of European legislation. As a result, not only does the Legal Service scrutinise more carefully the quality of the texts of the Parliament, it also checks the Councils common position. To do this work, Parliament established a service of "jurist linguists", which are translators with specialist legal knowledge, as it also exists already in the Commission, the Council and the ECJ (CORBETT et al 2000: 171).

Evaluating the role of the Legal service in providing direct parliamentary assistance for the Members of Parliament, one has to admit that their contribution is rather limited. This can be explained by the fact, that the Legal Service is spending much of its time in handling in legal cases on the behalf of the Parliament, and that these cases are increasing in number and complexity (CORBETT et al 2000: 171). As a result there is not much time left for a judicial assistance of legislative matters on specific subjects. Thus, the Legal Service tends to be rather an occasional help than providing permanent assistance for rapporteurs (NEUNREITHER 2002: 7)

4.1.2 Political and Private Assistance

4.1.2.1   The role of the Political Group Secretariats

Each political group has the right to establish their own secretariat, which is funded out of the general budget of the Parliament. There are precise rules regarding the numbers of staff to which Political Groups are allowed, depending basically on the number of members in each Group and also the number of working languages within the Group. Each group is entitled to a fixed total of two A grade (Administrative) posts, with a further two such posts for every 30 MEPs within the group, and another A grade post if the Group uses four or five languages, two posts for six or seven languages, etc. (CORBETT et al 2000: 82). The total number of posts per Political Group may not exceed the number of MEPs within that Group. The number of the staff of the Political Groups has grown in recent years in relation to the public service staff (CORBETT et al 2000: 172). In the year 2000, 532 posts were budgeted (of which 218 A grades) - as compared with 285 (of which 123 A grades) in 1982. This represents an increase of 87% (77% for A grades), as compared with 38% over the same period for Parliament's own staff (52% for A grades). This changed the balance between permanent officials recruited through open examinations and the political staff.

In the beginning, organisational tasks prevailed, but with the growing importance of legislation, these secretariats began to fulfil more directly supportive tasks for the legislative work of their members. The political group staff has today both general and sectoral responsibilities. Above all, they have the function to co-ordinate the activities of their own members during the committee deliberations and to prepare amendments in the name of their political group after adoption of a report in the committee and before its final discussion and vote in the plenary session (NEUNREITHER 2002: 9). Furthermore, they support the legislative work of their Group members through administrative or presswork, or responsibility for urgency debates in plenary. The political group staff has also the duty to prepare the discussions within their Group meetings, and help their members to formulate a Group position before the plenary session or may have to gather background information for the Group (CORBETT et al 2000: 85). Some staff work directly to assist the Group leader, whereas others follow particular policy areas. The larger groups are able to have one or two officials to follow each committee, whereas an official in a smaller Group may have to follow up to three or four committees at once. They assist their co-ordinators and help to ensure that the party line is as unified as possible by rounding up members from other committees to help in tight vote in meetings.

In order to evaluate the legislative assistance and advice capacity of the political group staff for their Members, one has to look as well at the number of A grade administrators and as also at what responsibilities these work forces have. The PES group for example has a staff of approximately 60 A grades totally. Yet only 30 of these do work "politically", that is on policy issues, the rest being busy with administrative tasks, financial duties, and human resources (Interview MERSCH 2002). This means for the PES group that they have only about one to two policy advisers per committee. These are then responsible for all dossiers that are treated in their respective committee, which is quite a lot. For an A grade who is responsible for the Economic and Monetary Committee this means for example that he works at the same time on competition policy, financial service legislation, economic policy, monetary policy etc. As a matter of fact, instead of being a real expert, the political group staff has rather to be a generalist in his policy area.

Furthermore, the role of these 'policy advisors' is to 70% of administrative, and only to 30% of political nature. These 30% of political duties consist to 15% in negotiation with the other political groups and to further 15% in giving "technical" input to MEPs (Interview MERSCH 2002). These figures put a light on how much of the available work force in terms of "heads" and time is really directly turning to account for legislative assistance and policy advice. One policy adviser of a political group stated that there is a huge lack of resources in the political group secretariats (Interview MERSCH 2002).

There seem to be some sort of competition between the "non-partisan" staff of the committee secretariats and the political staff of the groups in their legislative assistance of the rapporteur. The Group secretariats seek to be charged with the legislative assistance of "their" rapporteur. Yet, since the drafting of a whole report can be quite time consuming and demand expert knowledge, it has sometimes occurred that they asked the Parliaments Services, DG II and DG IV, to only provide a kind of background file which was then "politicised" by the responsible member of the political group secretariat (NEUNREITHER 2002: 9). However, these attempts to undermine to some extent the independent position of the committee secretariats failed. The growth in the powers of the Parliament has meant that both sets of staff have found themselves confronted with new challenges, with the Secretariat having to master, for example, the intricacies of the new co-decision procedure (CORBETT et al 2000: 172).

Thus, the political group secretariats, although increasing their role in co-ordination, have not played up to now a significant role in direct legislative assistance of rapporteurs (NEUNREITHER 2002: 10). This does not exclude, however, that they are busy preparing amendments for their members, both in the committee and in plenary. It does not make too much sense that the staff of the political groups provides for direct assistance of the MEPs of their group, because that is where national differences and backgrounds play an important role. Just to illustrate this point, one should imagine that for example a Spanish policy adviser specialised in environmental issues, should provide assistance for a German Member on environmental questions, yet because of their national background they have a very different perception of environmental problems. It is therefore reasonable to restrict the role of the political group secretariat to their original role which is to co-ordinate the political line of the group and guarantee coherence within the group voting within a committee and within the plenary.

4.1.2.2   The MEPs Private Staff

Each Member of the European Parliament is given a secretarial allowance to employ personal assistants[4], which they can employ with a considerable freedom. The role of these personal assistants varies greatly. Some are given considerable political responsibilities, while others concentrate more on office tasks. Typical tasks are to draft letters, articles, press releases or parliamentary questions, and to carry out background research. Some assistants help to draft reports when their boss becomes a rapporteur, but this still tends to be the exception. If, however, they are not generally called upon for drafting reports, they do frequently draft amendments. Brussels-based assistants also often attend meetings when their member is elsewhere engaged, and brief the member on what took place during their absence. In the early days of the directly elected Parliament the presence of assistants in Committee meetings was disputed in certain committees, but this is no longer the case. Today it is quite common that they attend committee meetings, being the "eyes and ears" of their member who is elsewhere engaged (CORBETT et al 2000: 112).

The allowance of the MEPs for private staff has recently been increased by 2000 Euro per month. This is enough to hire either additionally a full-time secretary or a part-time force with academic background. Today most of the Deputies have one assistant in their constituency and one and a half or two Brussels-based assistants. If you compare these numbers with those of the US Congress, where each deputy does have about 20-30 employees

---

[4] Members are actually given nearly 12.000 Euro a month by the European Parliament to cover staff costs (European Voice, 18–24 April 2002, Vol. 8, n. 15).

with academic background, the private assistance of the MEPs does rather seem poor. The US system allows the Congress deputies having for each policy field at least one assistant. This permits for the private staff to specialise in a single policy area and to develop a certain expertise in his/ her field of responsibility.

The private staff of the MEPs, which is providing for direct assistance and preparatory work for each Member is, in the eyes of several MEPs and the political group staff as well as the Vice-President, important and should therefore be increased. This is more so necessary as they are facing increased workload and time pressure.

4.1.3 The role of the Parliamentary Technology Assessment (STOA)

As a reaction on its ever larger role in legislation and its increased dependency on internal and external aid in form of independent expertise and policy advice necessary to fulfil its new competencies in the decision-making process, the European Parliament established in 1987 the STOA ("Scientific and Technological Options Assessment"), a TA capacity, to support that role. The creation of the STOA goes back to a report drawn up in 1985 for the Committee on Energy, Research and Technology (CERT) by a German Socialist MEP, Rolf LINKOHR, taking its inspiration from the Office of Technical Assessment (OTA) attached to the US Congress. When it was launched on March 26, 1987, it was a "project" under the aegis of CERT. In September 1988, the Bureau of the European Parliament extended the mandate of STOA, on condition that it widened the scope of its activities in a way as to serve all the committees of Parliament, and not just

CERT (HOLDSWORTH 2000: 200). Since then, STOA has been designed to be at the service of all committees requiring TA projects and to help Members of Parliament who increasingly find themselves in the position having to decide on matters with a scientific or technological component. It should however be noted that some committees have been more active in STOA than others partly due to nature of things.

The main task of STOA is to predict the possible impact of science and technology on society, economy and the environment and to assess policy options with pros and cons, which aim at assisting MEPs in making policy choices. It has furthermore the function to provide "early warning" of potentially negative consequences, especially unintended and indirect secondary effects that are not normally considered, when new technologies are deployed. Examples for such projects of the year 2001 have been "Production capacity of renewable energies in the EU", "Depleted uranium: Environmental and health effects in the Gulf War and in the Bosnia and Kosovo conflicts" or "The consequences of enlargement on EU agriculture". In addition to the production of long-term studies, STOA engages contractors to organise workshops and to write workshop reports on the basis of the presentations and discussions. These workshops provide an opportunity to bring experts, stakeholders, and European politicians and officials in a forum other than the formal policy-making setting of a committee or plenary session.

The STOA unit, which is situated in the Parliament's Directorate-General for Research (DG IV), is overseen at political level by the so-called STOA

Panel, which is composed of one[5] nominated member each from the twenty permanent committees of the European Parliament. The Panel adopts, on official request submitted by Parliament's committees, an annual work plan of projects proposed by the Committees. These projects are then executed with the assistance of outside contractors such as universities, research institutes and consultancies:

> "It is a key element of the philosophy of STOA specifically to seek high-quality, up-to-date expertise from outside the institutions of the European Union. This is consistent with the requirement that it should serve as a source of reliable, independent information and advice for the committees and members of the European Parliament (MEPs), whose principal task is the scrutiny of legislative and budgetary proposals coming from the European Commission" (HOLDSWORTH 2000: 199f.)

In preaching the doctrine of reliance on external expertise, STOA may be suspected of making virtue out of necessity, since the staff of the STOA unit has always been small with two A grades plus a number of trainees. Hence, instead of producing in-house studies as for example the POST (Parliamentary Office of Science and Technology) in the UK Parliament does, the work of the STOA staff consists essentially of managing an external research budget. This is not a problem per se. Even if the in-house staff of STOA were much increased, there would still be a need for external

---

[5] Except for the Committee on Industry, External Trade, Research and Energy and the Committee on the Environment, Public Health and Consumer Policy, which are allowed to have the right to be represented by two full members. (INTERNAL RULES OF PROCEDURE OF STOA, Art. 2)

contractors to be brought in for a significant work since it would be ineffi-
cient doing only in-house researches cut of the academic world:

"A TA agency working in a political institution having mainly other
objectives than research is in an entirely different situation. It has no
natural umbilical cord to the research community. If it attempted to
do all its work in-house then its researchers would have to work
twice as hard as their colleagues in national, academic environments
to maintain their links with the scientific community. There would
be no natural, unforced way for them to keep up to date with latest
developments" (HOLDSWORTH 2000: 217)

It should however be noted that, in order to guarantee good quality reports
and relative "independence" of expertise (if this is possible at all), the
STOA needs enough in-house expert staff in order to be capable to evaluate
the externally produced studies (Interview KARAPIPERIS 2002). The lack of
sufficient qualified human resources is thus one major weakness of the
STOA unit. Domestic capacity is yet urgently needed to manage and to filter the external expertise and also to make it readable and understandable
for the broad non-scientific public. Already the BOWE-Report from 1995
recommended establishing a credible internal and external quality control
procedure, to ensure that STOA reports are comprehensive, objective, ac-
curate, and relevant to the needs of its client, the Members of Parliament
and therefore to strengthen in-house capabilities (BOWE 1995: 4f).

The WESTERMEYER-Report of 1994, which undertook a detailed evaluation
of the work and role of STOA, showed clearly that continuing with STOA
in its earlier form would not meet the future needs of Parliament. This is
today even more so the case with regard to the growing number and complexity of scientific and technological options facing the European Parlia-

61

ment and by the prospect of an ever greater role of Parliament in the European legislation after Amsterdam.

The BOWE-Report on the future organisation of the STOA unit points out the importance of "political and administrative independence" of STOA - which in his eyes seems to be given - in order to ensure also the *scientific* independence of STOA's work (BOWE 1995: 5). It should however be noted, that some MEPs question the political independence of the STOA-Panel, which has the crucial function to decide, which projects are to be realised and which not. In fact, as it is up to the respective committees to design the Members of the STOA Panel, the composition of the latter does not reflect a proportional representation of political groups. Out of 19 members in total, the newly established STOA Panel is composed of 10 members from the EPP Group, 5 from the Greens/ EFA, only 3 from the PES group and 1 from UEN[6]. As a matter of fact, the choices of the Panel pro or contra specific projects cannot be described as completely politically neutral. There have been suspicions that certain requests have been rejected for political reasons (Interview MEP 2002).

Another important difficulty is timing, which is a crucial element in EU legislation and has become even more so since 1999 with the trend towards an ever-swifter conclusion of the co-decision procedure. The Committee Environment, Public Health and Consumer Policy wanted for example to know within one month time the impact of the Gulf War and in Bosnia and Kosovo on Environment and Health (Interview MERSCH 2002). There are thus very short time periods, especially in the Parliaments treatment of co-

---

[6] For more concrete information: http://www.europarl.eu.int/stoa/panel/comp_en.htm.

decision dossiers and an increasing demand for quick responses. Yet, the traditional in-depth studies of STOA take about 12 to 18 months, which is often too long (NEUNREITHER 2002: 10). The Project Cycle of STOA is per se too long as being able to provide short- and middle term studies.

Members of Parliament and Committee Presidents are since some years complaining in regard not only of STOA, but also of DG IV. They are pressing for a reform of both services in the sense of producing less "long-term studies" and concentrating more on "short-term briefings" (Interview ENGSTFELD 2002). It is also important to ensure that these "short-term briefings" are not too long, because MEPs, which are usually under great time pressure, simply don't read scientific studies that are longer than five to ten pages (Interview KAMP 2002). Apparently Parliament is slowly re-acting on this increasing request for quick responses and short term brief-ings, as recently a - rather vague - document on such a possible reform has been directed to the presidency of Parliament, which is however not pub-lic[7]. This is in any case an important area, where reforms of the STOA unit should be envisaged in order to improve the service for its client, the MEP, and support it in its legislative duties. A balanced mixture of quick re-sponses and in-depth studies seems to be necessary. The subjects must be planned far-sighted, along the Commissions multi-annual working plan, so that the studies are available early enough.

---

[7] Information gathered through e-mail request with an official of DG IV.

4.1.4 Conclusions

As the previous chapters have demonstrated, the European Parliament has at its disposal a certain variety of in-house services, on which Members of Parliament can rely, when they need support in their daily legislative work. Whereas DG IV and the STOA unit are providing for background information and expert knowledge on specific policy issues, DG II as well as the political and private staff assists MEPs directly in their legislative work. The European Parliament can thus certainly not be called completely powerless in this regard. However, compared with the in-house capacities of the US Congress, the European Parliament shows considerable structural weaknesses. The European Parliament also can't compete with the Commission in regard to the internal structures of research and expertise.

The European Parliament did not, and this is most serious, adapt its internal structures to the necessities growing out of its new role in European decision-making (Interview MERSCH 2002). As a result, it is not well equipped to tackle its new challenges. In order to fulfil well its new tasks and continue to seriously, the European Parliament should have increased its resources. However, it did not adapt to the new situation arising mainly from co-decision. Nothing has changed in respect to human resources over the last years. If you look at the number of A grades responsible for Committee, there is still the same number of persons, about 4-5 civil servants, as it has been pre-Maastricht (Interview MERSCH 2002).

Co-decision has to a certain extent exposed the Parliament's weakness in dealing with highly technical matters (PETERSON/ BOMBERG 1999: 44). The European Parliament lacks the resources in terms of expertise that e.g. the US Congress enjoy. Independent resources of expertise are however im-

64

portant, that the European Parliament can fulfil well its role in the legislative process. It is in the legislative field you see most that the resources are insufficient: when the Commission's legislative proposal, e.g. a directive reaches the European Parliament, one or two civil servants have been responsible for and dealing with this single proposal for one or two years, they have had contacts with all stakeholders like member states, lobbies and discussed the issue in their dense policy networks and "advocacy coalitions" (SABATIER 1998).

In contrast, one civil servant of the European Parliament works on approximately ten legislative dossiers (Directives) at the same time and one rapporteur has in most cases several reports to work on at the same time. So they do not at all have the necessary resources and capacities to reach the expertise and technical knowledge that Commissions civil servant can acquire over years. Since the Inter-Institutional Agreement of 1999 they have even less time to work on dossiers and to write reports. These developments, which led to the pressure for the European Parliament to work quicker on legislative proposals, should be equilibrated by an increase in personal resources, mainly A grades (Interview MERSCH 2002).

Also the Research Services of the European Parliament are not well adapted to the post-Maastricht and especially post-Amsterdam situation and necessities of the European Parliament. While DG IV and the STOA unit are available in providing background information in very general and basic questions with its long-term studies, there is definitely a major deficiency in the provision of short time briefings. They are not adapted to the immediate requirements of their clients, the MEPs. It is thus important that the internal services are revised in a way that they are more responding to the direct needs and the priorities of the deputies. A possible solution could be to provide for a mixture of quick and short briefings, on the one hand, and long-term studies, for more principle questions and the long development of a policy on the other.

Many Members of Parliament stated that there is a need for the creation of a genuine "Scientific Service" in the European Parliament that is functioning as the one in the German Bundestag, that is to say that MEPs can request short-term briefings, which are then delivered in short time periods (Interviews SCHMID, GEBHARDT, RÜBIG 2002). This has also been seen as a crucial innovation for the European Parliament in order to be to a certain degree autonomous from the expertise of the European Commission and also to include the newest scientific knowledge in the legislative process. It would be good, to make an inquiry among the Members of Parliament and ask them, which are their most important needs and then to adapt the internal structures and capacities to these requirements. It has first to be defined what are the basic needs of the Members of Parliament and then to adapt the internal structures to these demands.

4.2 External resources of expert knowledge

4.2.1 Hearings

Public Hearings are one of the main "instruments" of the European Parliament to seek outside expertise and advice and to enter into dialogue with interested parties. Some hearings bring together virtually the whole range of companies, trade unions and consumers concerned with a particular industry. Since its direct elections in 1979, Parliament's committees have held about 30 hearings a year. Hearings are usually conducted in the context of drafting a report, on behalf of a standing committee or of a committee of inquiry (CORBETT et al 2000: 272). This instrument became sometimes the object of quarrels between the political groups on the important questions whom to invite (NEUNREITHER 2002: 11). In most cases, they achieved, however to get a balanced invitation list.

It was, thus due to other reasons that hearings did loose some of their attractiveness after some time. Experts used to hold lengthy and detailed lectures, instead of transmitting theirs complete statements in written form in advance and use the ear-time of the deputies to answer concrete questions (NEUNREITHER 2002: 11). As hearings are very long, they often become boring for the majority of the Members of Parliament. Also due to the increasing legislative burden and the time-pressure of MEPs they often simply don't have the time to attend lengthy hearings. So, hearings have lost a bit of their original attraction.

4.2.2 The role of lobbying groups as resource of expertise

Whereas the traditional internal structures of legislative assistance remained rather the same despite the enhanced role of the European Parliament, the most dramatic changes have occurred during the last years in the field of interest representation. All sorts of interest groups, lobbyists, associations, individual enterprises, NGOs and consultants, have reacted to the increasing impact of the European Parliament in the EU decision-making process, following the "logic of influence". They have in such a way filled a vacuum, which evolved with the non-adaptation of the European Parliament's internal structures to the new situation. The interest groups did immediately react on the changing role of the European Parliament in European policy-making, as a consequence of the introduction of new legislative procedures and enhanced competencies.

Until the Single European Act (SEA), the Council and the Commission were the decisive players in European decision-making and have therefore been the main target of lobby groups, while the European Parliament had only advisory competencies and was hence not at all targeted by interest groups. With the introduction of the co-operation procedure in 1987 and especially the co-decision procedure with the Treaty of Maastricht, the European Parliament gained considerable attractiveness for interest groups and has since been more and more lobbied. The external pressure on the European Parliament, which comes also from the national industry, the national ministries and the domestic political parties, has been increased considerably. This enhanced effort that external actors put into the Parliament can be explained by the gain in salience and impact of the Parliaments work and decisions:

> "The lobbies are devoting more and more of their time to our deliberations. This is a good thing, a sign that we are no longer a talking shop, that the decisions we make affect the whole range of external interests" (BARÓN CRESPO 2000: 2).

There is a broad literature on the role of lobbies in the EU decision-making process. But only few studies deal with the role of interest representations for the European Parliament (KOHLER-KOCH 1997, SCHABER 1998, WESSELS, B. 1999). This study focuses mainly on the role of lobbies as a resource for expert knowledge for the European Parliament. Members of the European Parliament are on the average very open towards lobby groups and consider interest representation to be a matter of mutual benefit

(KOHLER-KOCH 1997: 10). Influence of lobbies goes with an interest group's capacity to provide what is most needed: technical expert knowledge. Indeed, information coming from interest groups is highly welcome by the Members of Parliament as they are dependent on technical and scientific expertise and advice. MEPs are mainly interested to get an assessment of the consequences of the European policy under consideration, but also in getting technical expertise, economic expert knowledge as well as policy advice on possible effects of a respective policy on public opinion.

The expert knowledge that the interest groups provide for, can be perceived as a "nice extra-service" to provide information and expert knowledge (SCHMID 2002). The lobbies have good papers, documents and prospects, which help to get a good identification of the problems and the key issues of a policy matter. They are very good in the description of the facts and circumstances, and of course they also lay down their proper interests as stakeholders in the issues. It is, however, important not only for the Members of Parliament, but also for the parliamentary assistants and officials, to make a *political* assessment of the different lobbies, to be critical and not to believe everything they tell us (KAMP 2002). It is thus important to evaluate well the context of the specific expert knowledge coming from lobbies and to detect critically the interests lying behind. In order to get a broad view and knowledge of the issue at stake, it is hence crucial that the MEPs consult all the different sides and stakeholders, as to say in concrete not only the industry lobbies but also the environmental NGOs, consumer associations and so on. Furthermore, Members of Parliament should not see interest groups as the only resource for information gathering, but rather as one among several, as their input is by its very nature politically biased and does represent particular interests.

However, due to the fact that the European Parliament is a pluralistic institution, where each interest has a certain right to be expressed, nobody can hinder an MEP, having an affiliation with for example the car-industry, to represent the particular interests of this branch only. However, such links have to be made transparent. Transparency is indeed a very important element in this respect, if the European Parliament wants to be credible. The Parliament has itself reacted on the increased pressure from interest representations and consultants in pushing for a regulation of lobbying in order to avoid abuses of lobbying and to eliminate unprofessional interest representation. The tendency to introspection met its apogee in 1991-92, in the aftermath of the negative Danish referendum on the Treaty of Maastricht (WESTLAKE 1994). The Rules Committee, which was asked to draw up a code of conduct and a public register for accredited lobbyists, emphasised on regulation rather than exclusion. There was, however, no consensus on what form this regulation should take and hence a broader debate was launched on questions like: if the MEPs should in highly technical matters be able to take over amendments drafted by lobbyists, or not? Or: in how far the Members of Parliament should disclose their financial interests.

The 1991 Galle report, which draws up a code of conduct and a register of lobbyists, and also pleaded for the disclosure of financial interests of the MEPs and the members' staff, has been rejected, as no consensus on these delicate issues was reachable. In 1994, with the Ford report, there has been another effort to move towards a regulation of lobbying. Its basic idea was to create a register, where interest representatives had to make their activities and interests public. They had to pay fees for their registration, to respect a code of conduct and to declare every year any benefits given to MEP, officials or assistants. In return they obtained a pass and access to parts of the European Parliament and to its documents. The report aimed at keeping transparency in the mutual relationship and to ensure that the system was not open to abuses:

> "The aim is not to restrict lobbying but, instead, to enable the European Parliament ... to have access to as much vital information as possible as can be gained from the lobbying process" (FORD 1995: 10f).

Finally, in 1996 a consensus on the question of regulating lobbying has been reached. With regard to the financial interests, each Members of the European Parliament is now required to make a detailed declaration of his professional activities and financial interests:

> "Au moment de prendre la parole devant le Parlement ou l'une de ses instances, tout députe ayant un intérêt financier direct dans l'affaire en discussion le signale oralement" (REGLEMENT 1999: 109, Annexe I, Art. 1). "Les questeurs tiennent un registre ou tout députe déclare personnellement et avec précision a.) ses activités professionnelles ainsi que toute autre fonction ou activité rémunérée, b.) les soutiens financiers, en personnel ou en matériel, venant s'ajouter aux moyens fournies par le parlement..." (RÈGLEMENT 1999: 109, Annexe I, Art. 2).

Interest representatives have to respect a code of conduct and to sign a register, which is made available to the public in all of the European Parliaments places of work. Lobbyists must carry a pass bearing their name at all times and produce a declaration listing all donations to Members of Parliament, their assistants and European Parliaments' staff (SCHABER 1998: 215). It was due to the immense national differences in cultural and judicial

71

attitudes towards lobbying that made it so difficult to find a compromise on how to regulate and cope with the increased interest representation at the European Parliament. But it also reflects an ideological difference, a conflict of values: political parties from the left, together with non-profit oriented interest groups, prefer stricter rules in order to restrict the superiority of industrial interests. Liberals and Christian-Democrats prefer an open dialogue without too much detailed regulation (SCHABER 1998: 216).

4.2.3 Other external possibilities to access expert knowledge

Apart form the internal capacities of the European Parliament and the lobby groups as important source of expertise, Members of Parliament have a high variety of other external possibilities to gather information and technical expert knowledge on specific policy issues. Members of Parliament have access to certain expert studies from the Commission, for example such that has been produced by the Joint Research Centre of the Commission (ISPRA) in Seville. This kind of expertise is however biased, as it has been produced for the Commission. Thus, it is not helpful for the Parliament, if it wants to present counter arguments to a Commission proposal.

When Members of the European Parliament face a new policy issue, on which they need technical knowledge and advice, their first step is often to consult their national ministries or national associations and interest groups, than relying on the European Parliaments formal internal sources of information. This could also be seen as an indicator for the insufficiencies of the European Parliaments internal structures and expertise resources.

Members of Parliament also receive their information from their own resources; for example from special experts and research institutes, which they know from their member state or region and in which they trust. MEPs argue that they trust more their own national expertise and institutes than those of others member states (Interview RÜBIG 2002). Some Members also go o the respective companies in order to consult themselves at place on the possible impacts of a Community policy on their industry branch. Members of Parliament have thus a lot of possibilities to access information and expert knowledge. The problem is, however, that the expert knowledge coming from external institutions is in most cases biased and thus not independent.

4.3 Conclusions

The European Parliament has a lot of possibilities to access external resources of information and expertise. The problem is thus not one of "access" to expertise, but rather one of independence and biased tendency. What the European Parliament lacks is thus not the quantity of access possibilities, but rather the necessary in-house evaluation and information gathering capacity. It needs thus to be better equipped with the workforce of qualified in-house staff, which is capable to filter and evaluate information and expertise coming in from outside.

There is a need for the European Parliament to have autonomous and resources of expertise, in order to be to a certain degree independent from the expertise of the Commission and private interest. It is true that the less in-house capacity the Parliament has, the more it gets dependent on external resources, which is always biased in one way or another. Parliament needs therefore a basic number of in-house capacities in order to evaluate the information and expertise coming in from external resources. There is a need of a certain degree of autonomy and independent expertise of the European Parliament from the Commission and the Council and also from the lobbies (Interview KARAPIPERIS 2002). Domestic capacity is needed to manage external knowledge, to filter the expertise coming in and to make it understandable for non-scientists.

One should know that no expertise is independent, as knowledge is always based on certain underlying assumptions, and that each expert is to a certain degree biased by his or her own interests. It is therefore seen as crucial by Members of the European Parliament to reflect as many as possible points of views and to evaluate each critically, being fully aware of the respective context and perspective of the information and expertise gathered (Interview GEBHARDT 2002). If one does know the background of the experts and if one does listen to all the different sides and stakeholders, this might however be a very helpful tool to get the basic expert knowledge, which is necessary to tackle a technical policy issue.

It is hard to measure the impact of the European Parliament on the legislative process and even more so to evaluate if the quality of expertise recruited by parliamentarians has an impact on the outcome of the legislative act. The impact of the Parliament on legislation can, however, be measured by the quantity of amendments that are accepted by the Council, and also by a qualitative analysis, which measures if the policy content has been influenced by the Parliaments' amendments. There are however opinions, which believe that the impact of the European Parliament on legislation depends more on the legislative procedure and on how persistent it acts in its negotiations with the Council than on the quality of the expertise gathered (Interview SCHMID 2002).

Nevertheless, the more informed Members of Parliament are on the policy issue and the more expertise they consulted, the more convincing they are in the bargaining process with the Council. As a result, it seems obvious that there is certain causality between the quality of expert knowledge of the European Parliament and their impact on legislation. The decision on the "silicon implants" does for example illustrates this relationship. It is a case, where Parliament has consulted a very broad range of expertise involving all kind of stakeholders and listening to and all the different positions: those who wanted to leave things as they were (industry), those who wanted to ban silicon implants (intergroup of women), and those who had an intermediate position wanting to continue, but improving the consultation of the patients. There has also been a STOA study on the subject. In this decision the European Parliament had a real policy impact on the legislation (Interview ENGSTFELD; Interview KARAPIPERIS 2002).

5 CONCLUSION

The starting point of this study has been the perception that the European Union is facing today more than ever a dilemma between technocracy and democracy. On the one hand, it is accused for its "democratic deficit" and the decline in parliamentary democracy. On the other hand, European policy-making is, as a result of its regulatory nature, highly dependent on expert knowledge and scientific advice. In Chapter two, it was argued that the real challenge for the European Union is thus to combine an increased politicisation with the need for more expertise. Politics and knowledge, which are normally seen as polar opposites, are indeed needed simultaneously for the development of public policy in the European Union.

The European Parliament, being the only directly legitimated body within the institutional set-up of the European Union and thus the democratic symbol, plays a key role in tackling the challenge of bridging the gap between technocracy and democracy. The European Parliament is the *political* institution that is marked by plurality and differing interests; and its duty it is to take political decisions on the policy issues. In such a way it adds a political and democratic element to the technocratic form of policy-making of the European Commission. The European Parliament plays therefore a major role in ensuring political control of the technocratic policy-making circles in the European Union, mainly through its responsibility in scrutinising the European Commissions legislative proposals. It is, however, becoming more and more difficult for Members of the European Parliament to understand and deal with the increasingly complex and sometimes highly technical matters. As a result, the European Parliament depends to a high degree on internal and external help in form of expert knowledge, policy advice and parliamentary assistance.

Chapter three demonstrated that the European Parliament has become in recent years an important player in the European Union decision-making process, especially as a result of the introduction of co-decision and its extension of scope in Amsterdam since it is now a genuine co-legislator alongside the Council. This gain in political power constitutes for the European Parliament a major challenge, as it has gone hand in hand with a parallel increase of responsibility for the legislation adopted or rejected and of workload to manage. With the simplification of the co-decision procedure in Amsterdam and the Joint Declaration of 4th May 1999, a tendency towards an ever-earlier closure of the procedure has become evident with the effect that the European Parliament has today also less time to form an opinion and work on a specific co-decision dossier. At the same time, as the integration process moved on, a series of new policy competencies have been transferred to the European level, among which highly technical and complex policy fields. As a result, the European Parliament, in addition to the challenge of its enhanced political weight, also has to deal with completely new and complex policy issues. Through this two-fold increase in power and in competencies, the European Parliament is also confronted with an inexorable increase in workload and responsibility. Furthermore, the issues at stake have become more and more technical and complex.

In order to tackle these new challenges and to play an influential role in European decision-making, Parliament depends to a high degree on its resources in terms of expertise, policy advice and parliamentary assistance. Chapter four therefore analysed the internal and external resources of the European Parliament in terms of expertise and policy advice structures. It was argued that the European Parliament, although being aware of the adaptation pressure, did not reform its internal structures, which are today still organised along the necessities of the pre-Maastricht era. As a result, it is not well equipped to work seriously, especially in technical policy issues. Although Members of Parliament have at their disposal various possibilities of support, like DG IV and the STOA unit for research studies, as well as DG II, private and political assistance for legislative assistance, these services have not been adapted to the direct needs of the MEPs since they have become genuine co-legislators besides the Council. Especially, the system of long-term studies provided by DG IV and STOA is not responding to the concrete needs of MEPs, who increasingly request for short-term briefings. Furthermore, despite the considerable increase in complexity, workload and time-pressure, there has not been a corresponding increase in terms of qualified human resources.

In contrast, dramatic changes have occurred in the field of interest representation. There has been a major increase in the efforts of lobby groups to influence the European Parliament. They reacted immediately to the gain in salience of the European Parliament with the introduction of co-decision. They did so with considerable success, as MEPs were keen to gain their technical expert knowledge. Interest representations have in such way filled a vacuum, which evolved with the non-adaptation of Parliaments' internal structures to the new needs of expertise and support. In other words: insufficient in-house capacities have made Members of Parliament more dependent on expertise gathered form outside and thus more captive for private interests.

Therein lies a serious danger for European democracy: if Parliament becomes dependent to a certain extent on the knowledge provided by private interests, but also by the Member States and the Commission, it is not capable of being an effective body of political control. In order to fulfil effectively its scrutiny function vis à vis the European Commission, it needs to be well equipped with independent information and knowledge structures. It is thus crucial for the European Parliament to guarantee a certain degree of autonomy and independence from the information and expertise coming from outside. The European Parliament needs therefore strong internal capacities and own structures of autonomous information and technical expertise.

As Andersen and Burns have rightly stated, there is today in the European Union a "gap between representative democracy's responsibility and its lack of structural capability and control" (ANDERSEN/ BURNS 1996: 243). The European Parliament, which is the representative body of the European Union, plays a key role in bridging this gap. As in today's society the complexity and difficulty of policy issues expand exponentially, independent resources of information and expert knowledge have become the key instrument for political institutions and organisations to be influential. If there is a way to rescue parliamentary democracy in the European Union, then it is certainly by equipping the European Parliament with these resources, which have become so fundamental in today's complex society.

6 INTERVIEWS

Interview with PAUL ENGSTFELD, Head of Division, DG IV Research, Brussels 5th March 2002.

Interview with THEO KARAPIPERIS, DG II, Committee Secretariat Industry and Technology, Brussels 25th March 2002.

Interview with EVELYNE GEBHARDT, Member of European Parliament, SPE, German, Brussels 20th March 2002.

Interview with Dr. GERHARD SCHMID, Member of European Parliament, SPE, German, Vice-President of the European Parliament, Brussels 17th April 2002.

Interview with PAUL RÜBIG, Member of European Parliament, PPE, Austrian, Brussels 17th April 2002.

Interview with MARCEL MERSCH, political adviser, Political Group Secretary of European Socialist Party, Brussels 25th March 2002.

Interview with MARTIN KAMP, political adviser, Political Group Secretary of European People's Party, Brussels 17th April 2002.

Interview with MICHAEL SHACKLETON, Head of Division in the Secretariat for the Conciliation Procedure, Brussels 15th April 2002.

7 BIBLIOGRAPHY

ANDERSEN, Svein S./ Kjell A. Eliassen (eds.) 1996: The European Union: How democratic is it? London.

ANDERSEN, Svein S./ Kjell A. Eliassen (eds.) 2001: Making policy in Europe.

ANDERSEN, Svein S./ Tom R. Burns 1996: The European Union and the erosion of parliamentary democracy: a study of post-parliamentary governance, in: Svein S. Andersen/ Kjell A. Eliassen (eds.) 1996↑, 227–251.

BARKER, Anthony/ B. Guy Peters (eds.) 1993: Advising West European governments. Inquiries, expertise and public policy, Pittsburgh.

BARKER, Anthony/ B. Guy Peters (eds.) 1993: The politics of expert advice. Creating, using and manipulating scientific knowledge for public policy, Pittsburgh.

BARÓN CRESPO, Enrique 2000: Is co-decision bridging the EU's democratic gap? Speech addressed to Friends of Europe, 16. October 2000.

BIMBER, Bruce 1996: The politics of expertise in Congress. Rise and Fall of OTA, New York.

BLOCK, Peter 1999: Flawless consulting: a guide to getting your expertise used, San Francisco 1999.

BÖRZEL, Tania A. 1998: Rediscovering Policy Networks as a Modern Form of Government, Journal of European Public Policy, 5, 2, pp. 354–359.

Bowe, David 1995: The Future organisation of the European Parliament's Programme for Scientific and technological options assessment (STOA), Draft Report to the President of the European Parliament, PE 184.202/rev.4, Strasbourg.

Caporaso, J. 1996: The European Union and forms of state: Westphalian, regulatory or post-modern?, in: Journal of Common Market Studies 34 (1), March, 29–52.

Clays, Paul-H./Corinne Gobin/ Isabelle Smets/ Pascaline Winand (eds.) 1998: Lobbying, Pluralism and European Integration.

Collingridge, D./ C. Reeve 1986: Science speaks to power. The role of experts in policy-making, London.

Collins/ Burns/ Warleigh 1998: Policy Entrepreneurs: the role of the European Parliament's Committees in the Making of EU Policy.

Consolidated Rules of Procedure of STOA, 25. Oktober 1999.

Corbett, Richard/ Francis Jacobs/ Michael Shackleton 2000: The European Parliament. Fourth Edition, London.

Costa, Olivier 2001: Le Parlement européen, assemblée délibérante, Bruxelles.

Costa, Olivier et al. (eds.) 2001: L'Union Européenne: une démocratie diffuse, in: Revue française de Science Politique, déc. 2001, vol. 51, n. 6, 859–948.

Council of the European Union 1999: Council Guide IV: Co-decision Guide, by the General Secretariat, September 1999.

COUNCIL OF THE EUROPEAN UNION 2000: Report by the Presidency and the General Secretariat of the Council to the European Council on making the co-decision procedure more effective, 13316/1/00 REV 1, Brussels, 28. November 2000.

CRAM, Laura 1997: Policy-Making in the EU. Conceptual Lenses and the Integration Process, London.

CRAM, Laura/ Desmond Dinan/ Neill Nugent 1999: Developments in the European Union, New York.

DAHL, Robert A. 1994: A Democratic Dilemma: System Effectiveness versus Citizen Participation, in: Political Science Quarterly, vol. 109, n. 1, 23–35.

DEHOUSSE, Renaud 1997: Regulation by networks in the European Community: the role of European agencies, in: Journal of European Public Policy 4 (2), June, 246–261.

DEHOUSSE, Renaud 1998: European institutional architecture after Amsterdam: parliamentary system or regulatory structure?, Robert Schuman Centre Working paper no. 11/98, EUI: Florence.

EUROPEAN PARLIAMENT 2000a: Activity Report 1 May 1999 to 31 July 2000, of the delegations to the Conciliation Committee presented by Vice-Presidents Renzo Imbeni, James Provan, Ingo Friedrich.

EUROPEAN PARLIAMENT 2000b: Conciliation Handbook, 2nd edition, by the Conciliation's Secretariat July 2000, 420330EN.doc.

EUROPEAN PARLIAMENT 2001: Note to the Conference of Presidents on Co-decision and conciliation, PE 302.715/BUR, Brussels 2001.

FISCHER, Frank 1990: Technocracy and The Politics of Expertise, London.

FISCHER, Frank 1993: Bürger, Experten und partizipatorische Policy Analyse, in: Politische Vierteljahresschrift 34 (Sonderheft 24), 451–470.

FORD, Glyn 1995: Report on the regulation of lobbying, European Parliament, Rules Committee, PE 212.311, 1995.

FOUCAULT, Michel 1980: Power–Knowledge – selected interviews and other writings 1972–1977, ed. by Colin Gordon.

GREENWOOD, Justin 1997: Representing Interests in the European Union, New York.

GREENWOOD, Justin/ Marc Aspinwall (eds.) 1998: Collective Action in the European Union. Interests and the new politics of associability, London/ New York.

HAAS, Ernst B. 1990: When Knowledge Is Power. Three Models of Change in International Organisations, Berkeley/ Los Angeles.

HAAS, Peter M. (ed.) 1992: Knowledge, Power and international policy coordination, in: International Organisation, Monographic Issue 46 (1): 367–390.

HAAS, Peter M. 1992: Epistemic Communities and international Policy Coordination, in: International Organisation 46, 1, pp. 1–35.

HABERMAS, Jürgen 1971: Knowledge and human interests, Boston.

HARCOURT, ALISON J./ Claudio Radaelli 1999: Limits to EU technocratic regulation?, in: European Journal of Political Research 35, 106–123.

HIX, Simon 1999: The Political System of the European Union, New York.

HOLDSWORTH, Dick 2000: Parliamentary Technology Assessment by STOA at the European Parliament, in: Vig/ Paschen 2000↑, 199–226.

HOPPE, Gerald W./ James A. Kuhlmann 1981: Expert generated data: applications in international affairs, Boulder.

JOERGES, C./ K. H. Ladeur/ E. Vos (eds.) 1997: Integrating scientific expertise into regulatory decision-making: National traditions and European innovations, Baden-Baden.

JOINT DECLARATION on practical arrangements for the co-decision procedure (Art. 251 of the EC Treaty) 1999, by European Parliament, Council and Commission, 1999/C 148/01, Strasbourg, 4 May 1999.

JUDGE, David/ Earnshaw, David/ Cowan: Ripples or Waves: The European Parliament in the European Community Policy Process, Journal of European Public Policy, Vol. 1, No. 1, 1994, pp. 27–51.

KATZ, Richard S./ Bernhard Wessels (eds.) 1999: The European Parliament, National Parliaments, and European Integration, Oxford.

KENNET, Lord 2000: Foreword, in: Vig/ Paschen 2000↑, vii–x.

KOHLER-KOCH, Beate 1997: Organised interests and the European Parliament, in: European Integration on-line Papers, http://eiop.or.at/.

KREPPEL, Amie 1999: What Affects the European Parliament's Legislative Influence? An Analysis of the Success of EP Amendments, in: Journal of Common Market Studies, Vol. 37, n. 3, 521–538.

LE GALES, P/ M. Thatcher (eds.) 1995: Les Réseaux de Politique Publique: Débat autour des 'Policy Networks', Paris.

LEQUESNE, Christian/ Philippe Rivaud 2001: Les Comités d'experts indépendants: l'expertise au service d'une démocratie supranationale ?, in : Revue Française de Science Politique, vol. 51, n. 6, déc. 2001, 867–880.

MAJONE, Giandomenico (ed.) 1990: De-regulation or re-regulation? Regulatory reform in Europe and the US, New York.

MAJONE, Giandomenico (ed.) 1996: Regulating Europe, London.

MARIN, Bernd/ Renate Mayntz (Eds.) 1991: Policy Networks. Empirical Evidence and Theoretical Considerations, Frankfurt a. M..

MARSH, D. (ed.): Policy Networks in Comparative Perspective.

MAZEY, Sonia/ Jeremy Richardson 1993: Lobbying in the European Community, Oxford/New York. (darin: Hull: a View from Within)

MIDDLEMAS, K 1995: Orchestrating Europe: the Informal Politics of the European Union 1997–1995, London.

MOSER, Peter 1996: A theory of conditional influence of the European Parliament in the co-operation procedure.

MOTHE, John de la 2001: Science, Technology and Governance, London.

NEUNREITHER, Karlheinz 1998: Der Vertrag von Amsterdam als Zwischenetappe der EU-Osterweiterung. In: Kirt, Romain (Hrsg.): Der Vertrag von Amsterdam - ein Vertrag für alle Bürger. [...]1998↑, 157–176.

NEUNREITHER, Karlheinz 1998: Governance without Opposition: The case of the European Union", in: Government and Opposition, vol. 33/4, 1998.

NEUNREITHER, Karlheinz 2000: Political Representation in the European Union: A Common Whole, Various Wholes, or Just a Hole? In: Neunreither, Karlheinz/Antje Wiener (Hrsg.): European Integration after Amsterdam [...] 2000↑, 129–151.

NEUNREITHER, Karlheinz 2001a: The European Union in Nice: A Minimalist Approach to a Historical Challenge, in: Government and Opposition, Vol. 36, Number 2, Spring 2001, pp. 184–208.

NEUNREITHER, Karlheinz 2001b: The Future of the EU: Has the European Parliament lost its Voice?, ECSA Seventh Biennial International Conference, May/June 2001, Madison, Wisconsin, unpublished.

NEUNREITHER, Karlheinz 2002: Elected legislators and their unelected assistance in the European Parliament, unpublished (to be published this year).

NEUNREITHER, Karlheinz/Antje Wiener (Hrsg.) 2000: European Integration after Amsterdam - Institutional Dynamics and Prospects for Democracy. Oxford.

NORRIS, Pippa 1997: Representation and the democratic deficit, in: Journal of Political Reseach 32, 273–282.

PARADISO, Anna-Cosima 1996: Expertise et évaluation face à la démocratisation du débat technico-scientifique dans une perspective européenne, Genève 1996.

PARSONS, David Wayner 1996: Public Policy. An Introduction to the Theory and Practice of Policy Analysis, Aldershot/ Lyne, SA.

PETERSON, John 1995: EU Research Policy: The Politics of Expertise, in: C. Rhodes/ S. Mazey (eds.) 1995↑, 391–411.

PETERSON, John 2000: Power, Decision and Policy in the European Union, Oxford.

PETERSON, John/ Elizabeth Bomberg 1999: Decision-Making in the European Union, New York.

PROGRAMMA MAATSCHAPPELIJK ONDERZOEK TECHNOLOGICAL ASSESSMENT 1994: De toegang tot expertise en informatieals probleem, Federale Diensten voor Wetenschappelijke, Technische en culturele Angelegenheden, Brussels.

RADAELLI, Claudio M. 1995: The role of knowledge in the policy process, in: Journal of European Public Policy 2 (2), 160–183.

RADAELLI, Claudio M. 1999: Technocracy in the European Union. Political Dynamics of the European Union, London/ New York.

REGLEMENT INTERIEUR DU PARLEMENT EUROPEEN 1999, 14ieme édition, juin 1999.

RHODES, C. 1997: Understanding Governance: Policy Networks, Governance, Reflectivity and Accountability, Buckingham.

RHODES, C./ S. Mazey (eds.) 1995: The State of the European Union vol 3: Building a European polity?, Harlow.

92

RHODES, R. A. W. 1997: Understanding Governance: Policy Networks, Governance, Reflectivity and Accountability, Buckingham.

RHODES, R.A.W./ I. Bache/ S. George 1996: Policy Networks and Policy-Making in the EU: A Critical Appraisal, in L. Hooghe (ed.): Cohesion Policy and European Integration, Oxford.

RHODES, R.A.W./D. Marsh 1990: New directions in the study of policy networks, in: European Journal of Political Research, vol 21.

RICHARDSON, Jeremy 1996: European Union: Power and Policy-Making, London.

RICHARDSON, Jeremy/ G. Jordan 1979: Governing under Pressure. Post-parliamentary Democracy.

SABATIER, P. A. 1998: The Advocacy Coalition Framework: Revisions and Relevance for Europe, in: Journal of European Public Policy 5, 1, 98–130.

SABATIER, P. A./ H. C. Jenkins-Smith (eds.) 1993: Policy change and learning. An advocacy coalition approach, Boulder.

SALOMON, J. J. 1973: Science and Politics, Cambridge.

SCHABER, Thomas 1998: The Regulation of lobbying in the European Parliament: The quest for transparency, in: Claeys et al. (eds.) 1998↑, 208–221.

SCLOVE, Richard 1995: Democracy and Technology, New York/ London.

SCULLY, Roger 1997: Policy Influence and Participation in the European Parliament, in: Legislative Studies Quarterly, vol 22, no. 2, 233–52.

93

SCULLY, Roger: Policy Influence and Participation in the European Parliament, Legislative Studies Quarterly, Vol 22, no. 2, 1997, pp. 233–52.

SHAPIRO, M. 1997: The problems of independent agencies in the United States and the European Union, in: Journal of European Public Policy 2 (1), 276–291.

STEUNENBERG, Bernard/ Frans van Vught (eds.) 1997: Political Institutions and Public Policy. Perspectives on European Decision Making, Dordrecht.

STONE, D./A. Denham/M. Garnett (eds.) 1998: Think tanks across the world. A comparative perspective, Manchester.

SUTHERLAND 1988: The Parliament and the Commission: partners or protagonists? in: Louis: Le Parlement Europeen dans l'évoution Institutionnelle.

TRONNER, Roman: Policy networks and new agendas: a comparative study of European socio-economic research.

VIG, Norman J./ Herbert Paschen (Eds.) 2000: Parliaments and Technology. The Development of Technology Assessment in Europe, New York.

WAARDEN, Frans von 1992: Dimensions and Types of Policy Networks, in: European Journal of Political Research 21, 1992, 29–52.

WALLACE, H/ A. Young (eds.)1997: Participation and Policy-Making in the European Union, Oxford.

WALLACE, W/ J. Smith 1995: Democracy or Technocracy. European integration and the problem of popular consent, in: West European Politics, vol. 18, no. 3, 1995, 137–57.

WALLACE/YOUNG 1997: Participation and Policy-Making in the European Union, Oxford.

WEAVER, R. K./ B.R. Rockman 1993: Do institutions matter? Government Capabilities in the US and Abroad.

WEILER, Tobias 1995: Das Europäische Parlament und die Forschungs- und Technologiepolitik in der Europäischen Union, Baden-Baden.

WEISS, C. H. 1979: The many meanings of Research Utilisation, in: Public Administration Review, 39 (5), 426–431.

WESSELS, Bernhard 1999: European Parliament and Interest Groups, in Katz/ Wessels (eds.) 1999↑, 105–128.

WESTERMAYER, Wiliam 1994: Evaluation du programme STOA Programme d'activité dans le domaine de l'évaluation des choix scientifiques et technologiques, Rapport au Parlement européen, PE 164.968, Luxembourg.

WESTLAKE, Martin 1994: A Modern Guide to the European Parliament, London.

WESTLAKE, Martin 1994: The Parliament and the Commission: Partners and Rivals in the European Policy-Making Process, London.

WITTRICK, B. 1982: Social knowledge, public policy and social betterment. A review of current research on knowledge utilisation in policy-making, in: European Journal of Political Research 10, no. 1, March, 83–89.

Brigitte Reck

Flexibilität
in der Europäischen Union

Entstehung und Entwicklung
eines alternativen Integrationsmodells

ISBN 3-89821-134-7
132 S., Paperback
29,90 €

Erhältlich in jeder Buchhandlung oder direkt bei
ibidem

Die Europäische Union steht heute angesichts der bevorstehenden Erweiterung um zehn postkommunistische Staaten Mittel- und Osteuropas sowie Zypern und Malta vor großen Herausforderungen und Entscheidungen. Die mit der Ausdehnung einhergehende Steigerung der Heterogenität der Gemeinschaft nicht nur bezüglich der wirtschaftlichen Leistungskraft, sondern auch hinsichtlich der politischen Interessenlagen wird es zunehmend schwieriger machen, auf der Basis des einstimmigen Konsens neue Integrationsfortschritte zu erzielen. In diesem Zusammenhang stellt sich die Frage, ob die bisher geltende einheitliche Integrationsmethode, die Jean Monnet in den fünfziger Jahren für jene relativ homogene Sechsergemeinschaft der Gründerstaaten kreiert hat, in einem "großen Europa" mit voraussichtlich 27 Mitgliedstaaten noch aufrechterhalten werden kann.

Brigitte Reck thematisiert daher in ihrem vorliegenden Buch mit Blick auf die anstehende Expansion der Europäischen Union Flexibilität als alternative Integrationsmethode zur bisherigen. Unter der leitenden Frage nach der faktischen Bedeutung von Flexibiltät für den Integrationsfortschritt der Gemeinschaft werden sowohl die theoretischen Beiträge zur Debatte untersucht - von den Vorschlägen einer Abstufung der Integration, wie sie beispielsweise von Willy Brandt in den 70er Jahren vorgetragen wurden, bis hin zur Kerneuropa-Konzeption des Schäuble-Lamers-Papiers - als auch konkrete Beispiele differenzierter Integration aus der politischen Praxis der EU, wie zum Beispiel die Wirtschafts- und Währungsunion. Schließlich werden die in Amsterdam eingeführten und in Nizza revidierten Bestimmungen über eine verstärkte Zusammenarbeit, mit denen erstmals Flexibilität als generelles Prinzip im Vertrag verankert wurde, auf ihren Nutzen für die Dynamisierung des europäischen Einigungsprozesses hin analysiert.

Die Autorin: Brigitte Reck studierte Politikwissenschaft und Germanistik an der Universität Heidelberg und dem Institut d'Études Politiques in Paris und absolvierte ihren Master of European Studies am Europakolleg in Brügge. Zur Zeit arbeitet sie als wissenschaftliche Mitarbeiterin im Europäischen Parlament in Brüssel.

Internationalisierung substaatlicher Regionen

Wettbewerb der Regionen in einer
globalisierten Welt
– eine vergleichende Analyse
der Außenwirtschaftspolitik von
Baden-Württemberg und Niedersachsen

ISBN 3-89821-229-7

168 S., Paperback, € 32,00

Erhältlich in jeder Buchhandlung
oder direkt bei

ibidem

Internationalisierung, Globalisierung und Regionalisierung sind Begriffe, die in den zurück-liegenden zwei Jahrzehnten reichlich Stoff zur Diskussion gegeben haben. Volkswirtschaft, Politik und die Medien erörtern die Auswirkungen dieser Prozesse auf die Gesellschaft. Welche Implikationen ergeben sich jedoch durch diese auf substaatlicher Ebene? Auf der Grundlage aktueller politikwissenschaftlicher Theorien untersucht Oliver Kämpf die Außen-wirtschaftspolitik der beiden Bundesländer Baden-Württemberg und Niedersachsen.

Die Theoriedebatte erörtert die gängigsten Ansätze, die entweder den Staaten Hand-lungsmöglichkeiten absprechen und diese allenthalben auf der internationalen Ebene se-hen, ebenso wie staats- bzw. politikzentrierten Ansätze. Zu den besprochenen theoreti-schen Erklärungsansätzen gehören die dominierenden Ansätze der Globalisierung und In-ternationalisierung. Zum dritten werden mögliche strategische Ausrichtungen substaatlicher Einheiten in Form des Private-Public-Partnership und des Global-Governance-Konzepts dargestellt.

Im empirischen Teil analysiert und vergleicht Oliver Kämpf auf der Basis von Primärquellen die beiden Bundesländer im Bereich der Außenwirtschaftspolitik und Strukturdaten. Das Regierungshandeln, beteiligte Institutionen, die rechtliche Verfassung und die Exportstruk-turen werden anhand vieler Schautafeln und Abbildungen dargestellt. Für die Beantwortung der Forschungsfrage „Wie wirkt sich wirtschaftliche Internationalisierung auf substaatliche Regionen aus?" werden die folgenden methodischen Verfahren angewendet: a) quantitati-ve Messung des Internationalisierungsgrads, b) qualitative Analyse der politischen Anpas-sung, c) historische Betrachtung und Entwicklung von Politikstilen.

Der Anhang bietet einen Überblick über Außenwirtschafts-Förderprogramme der Bundes-länder und die wichtigsten Internetadressen zur Außenwirtschaft.

Der Autor

Oliver Kämpf, Jahrgang 1972, studierte Politikwissenschaft mit Schwerpunkt Internationale Politik und Germanistik an der Universität Stuttgart. Er ist derzeit wissenschaftlicher Mitar-beiter im deutschen Bundestag.

Die Publikation wurde durch den Förderverein Politikwissenschaft an der Universität Stutt-gart e.V. (FöPS) gefördert.

Robert Woggon

Der Versuch, Schilf in der
Wüste zu pflanzen

Europäisch-palästinensische
Entwicklungszusammenarbeit
von 1993 bis 2002

ibidem

Robert Woggon

Der Versuch, Schilf in der Wüste zu pflanzen

*Europäisch-palästinensische
Entwicklungszusammenarbeit
von 1993 bis 2002*

ISBN 3-89821-222-X
196 S., Paperback, € 26,00

Erhältlich in jeder Buchhandlung oder direkt bei

ibidem

Das vorliegende Buch geht von folgenden Grundgedanken aus:
Es ist notwendig, alle wichtigen direkt oder indirekt in den Aufbau involvierten Akteure in die Darstellung mitein zu beziehen, namentlich Israel, die Palästinensische Autonomieverwaltung (PNA)
und die Gebergemeinschaft. Die israelische Politik gegenüber den Autonomiegebieten hat einen
großen Einfluss auf den Aufbauprozess, ebenso wie die Wirtschafts- und Sozialpolitik der PNA oder
die Strategien der Entwicklungszusammenarbeit (EWZ) der Geber.
Aufgrund der Größe der Gebergemeinschaft musste aus ihrer Mitte ein Fallbeispiel gewählt werden.
Die Entscheidung für die Europäische Union ist hierbei sinnvoll, da diese nicht nur aufgrund ihres
ausgeprägten Engagements sondern auch aufgrund eines spezifischen Interesses an einem Aufbau der Autonomiegebiete eine besondere Position innerhalb der Gebergemeinschaft hat.
In Anlehnung an diese Grundgedanken ist das Buch in sechs Abschnitte gegliedert, die die folgen-
den Fragen hinsichtlich des Aufbauprozesses beantworten sollen:
• Welcher sozio-ökonomische Entwicklungsstand und welche Strukturen lagen in den palästinensischen Gebieten zum Zeitpunkt der Prinzipienerklärung vor und welche Anforderungen stellte
  dies an den zukünftigen Aufbauprozess?
• Wie sollte sich die weitere israelisch-palästinensische Zusammenarbeit gemäß der bilateralen
  Folgeverträge gestalten und welche Chancen und Risiken ergaben sich daraus für den Aufbauprozess?
• Wie gestaltete sich die finanzielle und technische EWZ zwischen der Gebergemeinschaft und
  der Palästinensischen Autonomieverwaltung und inwieweit wurde diese den herausgestellten
  Anforderungen gerecht?
• Welches Interesse und welchen Anteil hatte explizit die Europäische Union am Aufbauprozess
  in Palästina?
• Welche sozio-ökonomische Situation zeigte sich nach sieben Jahren intensiver Aufbauarbeit,
  wie haben die drei genannten Akteure diese Situation mitverursacht, und welche Rückschlüsse
  lassen sich daraus für den langfristigen Erfolg des Aufbauprozesses ziehen?
• Wie entwickelte sich die Al-Aqsa-Intifada seit dem Herbst 2000, welche sozio-ökonomischen
  Konsequenzen hatte sie bislang für die Autonomiegebiete und welche Schritte wurden bislang
  unternommen, um ihr entgegenzuwirken?

Der Autor:

Robert Woggon hat an der Westfälischen Wilhelms-Universität Münster Politikwissenschaft, Neuere
und Neuste Geschichte und Soziologie studiert. Während eines dreimonatigen Aufenthaltes im
Gaza-Streifen hatte er 1999 Gelegenheit, die Entwicklungsproblematik in den palästinensischen
Autonomiegebieten täglich selbst zu erfahren.

Sven Engel

Vom Elend der Postmoderne in der Dritten Welt

Eine Kritik des Post-Development-Ansatzes

ISBN 3-89821-128-2
170 S., Paperback
EURO 25,00

Erhältlich in jeder Buchhandlung oder direkt bei *ibidem*

Kurzbeschreibung

Postmoderne - Entwicklung - Dritte Welt. In diesem begrifflichen Dreieck bewegt sich das Buch von Sven Engel. Der Autor führt in die Geschichte der Entwicklungstheorie ein, diskutiert die Machtanalytik von Michel Foucault und verfolgt eine kritische Darstellung des Post-Development-Ansatzes, der sich auf postmoderne und poststrukturalistische Theorien bezieht.
Aus Sicht dieses neuen Ansatzes dient der Entwicklungsdiskurs der vergangenen Jahrzehnte als Instrument der Herrschaft über die sogenannte Dritte Welt: Zuschreibungen wie "Entwicklung" und "Wachstum" konstituieren diese Dritte Welt erst und normieren, verwalten und unterdrücken sie. Die Mechanismen von Objektivierung, Professionalisierung und Institutionalisierung in der aktuellen Entwicklungsdebatte spielen dabei die zentrale Rolle der Unterdrückung. "Entwicklung" stellt somit ein diskursiv konstruiertes System der Kontrolle dar, in dem die betroffenen Menschen in den "Entwicklungsländern" gefangen sind.
Widerstand kann in den Vorstellungen von Post-Development nur an den Grenzen dieses Systems gelingen, in der Vielfalt kleiner Alternativen, die an indigene Tradition anknüpfen und für kommunale Besonderheiten und Genderfragen offen sind.
Sven Engel gelingt es, diesen auf den Theorien von Foucault und Lyotard beruhenden Ansatz kritisch darzustellen und in das Umfeld von Postkolonialismus, feministischer Entwicklungskritik und kulturwissenschaftlichen Perspektiven einzuordnen. Er zeigt aber auch auf, wie die Widersprüche des postmodernen Denkens, seine normative Kriterienlosigkeit und die mangelhafte Berücksichtigung materieller Grundlagen auf den Post-Development-Ansatz rückwirken. Das Elend der Postmoderne in der Dritten Welt besteht somit in den politisch fragwürdigen Konsequenzen von einer postmodernen Entwicklungskritik.

Über den Autor

Sven Engel, geboren 1973 in Basel, studierte Politische Wissenschaft an der Freien Universität Berlin. Seit seiner Zivildienstzeit in einem Obdachlosenprojekt in Chicago interessiert er sich für Fragen von Armut, Weltwirtschaft und sozialer Ungerechtigkeit. Den Anstoß zur vorliegenden Arbeit gab seine Mitarbeit bei SWADHINA, eine entwicklungspolitische Grassroots-Initiative in Kalkutta. Wissenschaftlich beschäftigt er sich mit politischen und ökonomischen Theorien, der Kritik von Entwicklungspolitik und den Problemen internationaler Beziehungen.
Zur Zeit arbeitet er für die Fraktion der Vereinigten Europäischen Linken im Europäischen Parlament zu Themen von Migration, Asyl, und europäischer Entwicklungspolitik.

Bestellungen und Anfragen richten Sie bitte an den

ibidem-Verlag, Melchiorstr. 15, 70439 Stuttgart, Tel.: 0711 / 9807954, Fax: 0711 / 8001889

ibidem@ibidem-verlag.de

www.ingramcontent.com/pod-product-compliance
Lightning Source LLC
Chambersburg PA
CBHW050539270326
41926CB00015B/3300